Bruce Nicholls

From Groaning to Liberation

The WEA Global Issues Series

Editors:

Thomas Schirrmacher

Secretary General, World Evangelical Alliance

Bishop Efraim Tendero, Philippines

Global Ambassador of World Evangelical Alliance

Volumes:

1. Thomas K. Johnson – Human Rights
2. Christine Schirrmacher – The Islamic View of Major Christian Teachings
3. Thomas Schirrmacher – May a Christian Go to Court?
4. Christine Schirrmacher – Islam and Society
5. Thomas Schirrmacher – The Persecution of Christians Concerns Us All
6. Christine Schirrmacher – Islam – An Introduction
7. Thomas K. Johnson – What Difference does the Trinity Make
8. Thomas Schirrmacher – Racism
9. Christof Sauer (ed.) – Bad Urach Statement
10. Christine Schirrmacher – The Sharia: Law and Order in Islam
11. Ken Gnanakan – Responsible Stewardship of God's Creation
12. Thomas Schirrmacher – Human Trafficking
13. Thomas Schirrmacher – Ethics of Leadership
14. Thomas Schirrmacher – Fundamentalism
15. Thomas Schirrmacher – Human Rights – Promise and Reality
16. Christine Schirrmacher – Political Islam – When Faith Turns Out to Be Politics
17. Thomas Schirrmacher, Thomas K. Johnson – Creation Care and Loving our Neighbors: Studies in Environmental Ethics
18. Thomas K. Johnson (Ed.) – Global Declarations on Freedom of Religion or Belief and Human Rights
19. Thomas Schirrmacher, David Schirrmacher – Corruption
20. Christine Schirrmacher, Thomas Schirrmacher – The Oppression of Women: Violence – Exploitation – Poverty
21. Christine Schirrmacher – Islam and Democracy
22. Amanda Jackson, Peirong Lin (Ed.) – Co-workers and co-leaders Women and men partnering for God's work
23. Bruce Nicholls – From Groaning to Liberation A Christian response to creation care and climate change

"The WEA Global Issues Series is designed to provide thoughtful, practical, and biblical insights from an Evangelical Christian perspective into some of the greatest challenges we face in the world. I trust you will find this volume enriching and helpful in your life and Kingdom service."

Bruce Nicholls

From Groaning to Liberation

A Christian response to
creation care and climate change

WIPF & STOCK · Eugene, Oregon

Wipf and Stock Publishers
199 W 8th Ave, Suite 3
Eugene, OR 97401

From Groaning to Liberation
A Christian response to creation care and climate change
By Nicholls, Bruce
Copyright © 2022 Verlag für Kultur und Wissenschaft Culture and Science Publ.
All rights reserved.
Softcover ISBN-13: 978-1-6667-4434-7
Hardcover ISBN-13: 978-1-6667-4435-4
Publication date 4/5/2022
Previously published by Verlag für Kultur und Wissenschaft Culture and Science Publ., 2022

Dedication

To Julie Belding

A faithful co-editor

Lawrence Ko

An environmental activist for the kingdom of God

The late Ken Gnanakan

A pioneer in motivating others to care for God's creation

Contents

Introduction

Planet Earth is changing and all of life is under attack. One fact is clear: the global climate is changing faster than scientists anticipated. The result is that both human beings and animals are suffering, and their suffering is increasing globally.

Some questions we need to discuss are: Is this change the consequence of cyclic climatic factors, or is it the consequence of human action? Are we reaching the "tipping point," as some scientists are warning, so that costly and drastic action is needed? Are we justified in spending billions of dollars to drastically reduce the level of carbon dioxide in the air in order to save the planet from self-destruction? Or should we also be building up our re-sources in order to adapt to climate crises such as floods and droughts, rising sea levels and water shortages? The different responses to these questions will be discussed in this book.

Sally McFague[1] shares her own response:

> "Climate change, quite simply, is the issue of the twenty-first century. It is not one issue among many, but, like the canary in the mine, it is warning us that the way we are living on the planet is causing us to head for disaster. We must change. All of the other issues we care about—social justice, peace, prosperity, freedom—cannot occur unless our planet is healthy. It is the uni-fying issue of our time."

Are there several ways of liberating Planet Earth from its bondage? We will explore the options. Most scientists and environmentalists attribute global warming to the increase in the use of fossil fuels which release carbon di-oxide and other gases into the atmosphere, resulting in serious weather disturbances.

But statistics may be misleading. Not all scientists agree with the causes of climate change. A minority are sceptical about this "point of no return." They believe climate change is cyclic, involving both long-term cycles, as in several Ice Ages, and short-term cycles, as in modern times. Further-more, they believe climate change is due more to the changes in the sun's radiation, and the level of water vapour, cloud coverage and volcanic ac-tivity, than to the changing levels of greenhouse gases. The IPCC scientists either refute the views of the sceptics or ignore them altogether.

---

[1]   Sally McFague, *A New Climate for Theology: God, the World, and Global Warming* (For-tress Press, 2008)

Perhaps the most disturbing factor is that change has escalated in the past thirty years, and appears to be doing so at an ever-faster rate. Weather patterns are becoming more extreme, as seen in floods and cyclones, droughts and bushfires. A new level of open-mindedness is needed if people are going to respond to what in reality are moral issues, calling for moral answers.

Climate change has become a religion, especially for those with no religious faith. In this study we discuss the difference between "alarmists" and "sceptics." The former fear that 2050 will be the tipping point of no return, while the latter consider factors other than carbon dioxide, both natural and human, to be causing global warming and climate change. Unfortunately, there appears to be little hope of a middle ground.

Both human and natural causes need more analysis and debate in order to clarify the options and to plan for a more sustainable society. Whatever course we follow calls for painful and costly sacrifices. In reality, few individuals, communities and nations, are willing to change to a simpler and more moral lifestyle in order to save the planet from further abuse and decline.

The title *From Groaning to Liberation* is taken from Paul's letter to the church in Rome (Romans 8:18-27) in which he says creation is "groaning as in the pains of childbirth." It is subject to frustration and bondage to decay, waiting to be liberated by the Spirit of God, through the people of God, into a glorious freedom. Paul's message is one of judgment for abuse and one of hope for both Planet Earth and all of its creation. This is because God the creator and sustainer of all things "will reconcile to himself all things by making peace through his blood shed on the cross." (Colossians1:20). This is yet to be fulfilled, but for the Christian there is no doubt it will be at some time in the future. Despite the fear that the worst is still to come, we are committed to the hope of the ultimate liberation of creation.

Chapter 1: The Human Factor in Climate Change

The world scientists' warning to humanity: a second notice

In 1992 the Union of Concerned Scientists and 1700 independent scientists published a manifesto: the *World Scientists' Warning to Humanity* in which they showed that human beings were on a collision course with the natural world. They declared that humanity was pushing the earth's ecosystem "beyond its capacity to support the web of life." On the 25th anniversary, November 13, 2017, they published *World Scientists' Warning to Humanity, a second notice*[2]. Fifteen thousand, three hundred and sixty-four scientists from 184 countries endorsed it. They declared humanity had failed to make sufficient progress in solving the environmental changes, In fact, the global situation was worsening, They pointed to the challenge of the rising greenhouse gases (GHGs) due to the burning of fossil fuels, deforestation, ruminating farm animals, collapsing biodiversity and the exploding human population which had increased by two billion since 1992.[3] The scientists called on governments to take immediate action, as a moral imperative.

The Concerns of the IPCC and the Paris 2015 Agreement

In 1988 the Intergovernmental Panel on Climate Change (IPCC) was created by the UN Environment Programme and the World Meteorological Organisation. The IPCC has the support of 195 member countries. It does not conduct its own research but seeks to identify agreement in the scientific community, and where further research is needed.

On 12 December 2015 the Paris Agreement was adopted by 196 partners and became legally binding on 4 November 2016. Its goal was to limit the increase in global warming to below 2° C, and if possible, to 1.5 °C, above the level at the time of the industrial revolution in the 1850s. Each country agreed to submit its plans for climate action every five years. The goal was

---

[2] https://academic.oup.com/bioscience/article/doi/10.1093/biosci/bix125/4605229.
[3] Ibid.

to achieve zero carbon increase by 2050. If this were not met, members feared that the earth would reach "a tipping point of no return" with increasingly destructive consequences for humanity and the environment. Their concern was the escalation of fossil fuel carbon emissions since the 1980s. In the 1850s, carbon was 280 parts per million (ppm). In 1960 it was 313 ppm, and in 2021 it was 419 ppm.

In 2018 the IPCC published a special report on the danger of global gas emissions reaching 1.5° C above preindustrial levels. The report outlined three concerns: the strength of the global response, the need for sustainable development, and the eradication of poverty. It estimated that the level of global warming had increased by 1°C above preindustrial levels, and of this, 87% of 1 degree had increased between 2006 and 2015. The rapid increase of CO_2 during the same period is assumed to be the main cause of the increase in global temperatures.

It is assumed that the use of fossil fuels is a major factor in the rise of global temperatures. It is significant that solar radiation modifications are not included in the report. Noncarbon radiating forces are recognised but are not considered an important cause of global warming. The report fears that an increase in global warming of 2° will result in massive weather disturbances including droughts, flood, cyclones, rising sea levels, ocean acidity and the partial extinction of biodiversity.

The fossil fuel crisis

As noted above, the IPCC and the reports of the Paris Agreement claim the earth is on a collision course with the natural world.

The global climate is changing faster than scientists anticipated. It is the unifying crisis of the 21st century. They say the resolution of all other issues such as freedom, peace, prosperity and justice in society depends on a stable and healthy climate. For many secular people, the restoring of climate equilibrium has become a religious faith, overshadowing all other concerns.

The IPCC and its supporters, including scientists, environmentalists and politicians, claim the primary cause of climate instability is the increasing use of fossil fuels—coal, oil and gas, particularly coal—as the dominant element of the GHGs. There has been considerable success in eliminating the mining of coal in the developed nations. In New Zealand, for example, the mining of coal for domestic and industrial use has almost stopped, with the belief that electricity will be produced by hydro, wind and solar power. Unfortunately, in 2019 New Zealand found it necessary to import a million tons of lower-grade coal from Indonesia to meet the increasing need for electricity.[4] It can be assumed that the production of steel and cement will require coal-burning furnaces for many years to come.

It is not expected that the demand for oil will lessen in the near future. Every year, transport by road, sea and air is increasing globally. The development of electric cars and trucks in several developed nations is to be commended, and China is the pioneer in this field. Unfortunately, it will be many years before lower-income families can afford such a car and there will always be a worldwide demand for cheap, second-hand petrol-driven vehicles – the kind that are driven in most Asian countries. In India, I often observed a middle-class family of parents and two children travelling on one petrol-driven motor cycle or scooter. Traffic jams in the major cities of the world consume even more petrol.

Before the Covid 19 pandemic, cruise ships with from 1,500 to 5000 passengers would berth each week in Auckland. In their global travels they could use up to 250 tons (around 80,000 gallons) of fuel per day.[5]

The use of natural gas is more hopeful. LPG (liquid petroleum gas) has a less detrimental effect on climate change than either coal or oil, but has a limited use in the automobile industry. Pipelines transport natural gas from one country to another, for example, Russia exports gas to Germany and other European countries. Likewise, pipelines from Siberia supply the US markets.

While there are hopeful signs that developed countries in the western world can achieve zero carbon increase by 2050, this will not happen in the undeveloped world where 70 percent of the global population live. Small nations such as New Zealand, with a population of 5.5 million, expect to reach zero carbon increase between 2030 and 2050. While New Zealand's influence on the level of global carbon is miniscule, it sets an example to the developing world.

The IPCC emphasises that the emission of greenhouse gases, particularly CO_2, increases the density of the shield of gases surrounding the earth at the levels of both the troposphere and the stratosphere. This reduces the amount of solar energy radiating back into space. As a result, both the earth's surface and the atmosphere become warmer. But to maintain an equilibrium in this process (with zero increase in carbon) is essential for life on planet earth. Without this shield the earth's surface would cool to at least -18° C and become like that of Mars. Also, the present increase in

---

[4]   See   https://www.rnz.co.nz/news/national/446845/nz-imported-more-than-a-million-tonnes-of-dirty-coal-last-year.

[5]   https://cruises.lovetoknow.com/wiki/How_Much_Fuel_Does_a_Cruise_Ship_Use.

CO_2 has a beneficial effect in the greening of nature. For example, some farmers in developed nations even inject bottled CO_2 into their glasshouses to improve plant production.

The IPCC report of 2021 is less confident about reaching the global target by 2050. It states that despite governments reaching their goals, "it is more likely than not" an increase 1.5 degrees Celsius will be reached by 2050.

The role of methane emissions

Next to carbon dioxide, methane is the second most important contributor to GHGs, from 4 to 9 percent, and it is increasing. Thought it is a minor issue, it is 25 times more potent than CO_2. It lasts only a few days, but its influence should not be underestimated. Forty percent of methane emissions are from natural sources and sixty percent are from anthropogenic (human) sources.[6] The main natural sources of methane are: wetlands (75 percent), ruminating animals (mainly cattle and sheep), decomposing organic material in landfills, melting permafrost in the Arctic tundra, and a small amount from the oceans. Human-generated methane sources include the burning of fossil fuels, landfills, coal mining and leakage from gas processing and distribution pipelines. Methane is steadily increasing from the growing motor vehicle industry and also from the rice paddy fields. One reason methane is less influential in raising the global temperature is that it is short-lived—just days compared with carbon dioxide which lasts for many years.

The influence of water vapour

The water in oceans, lake and rivers covers 70 percent of the earth's surface and therefore is an important factor in regulating the earth's temperatures. According to NASA, water in the form of water vapour comprises 36 to 70 percent of the greenhouse gases that surround the earth, while carbon dioxide comprises 9 to 20 percent, methane 4 to 9 percent, and ozone 2 to 7 percent.[7] Together their influence has been increasing since the 1850s and noticeably over the last 40 years. These gases including water vapour, create a shield around the earth. The sun's radiation hits the earth and bounces back to the shield of gases which return it to the earth, thereby warming it.

---

[6]   https://en.wikipedia.org/wiki/methane_emissions.
[7]   https://en.wikipedia.org/wiki/Greenhouse_effect, p. 3/8.

As the oceans and lakes warm, in part from the rising temperature of the earth, the level of water vapour increases and become a major component of the greenhouse gases, though its influence is believed to be less than that of carbon dioxide. One reason for this is that water vapour stays in the atmosphere for a shorter period, days compared with the years of CO_2. The rising level of water vapour intensifies the GHG shield around the earth. One estimate is that water vapour feedback is most likely responsible for the doubling of the greenhouse effect.[8]

However, the influence of the greenhouse gases on the temperature of the oceans is small compared to the direct influence of the sun's radiation which changes as the tilted earth revolves around the sun.

Clouds have an important influence on both the warming and the cooling of the atmosphere. As the clouds form from the increased water vapour, they block the sun's radiation from reaching the earth. Hence the earth's temperature is cooled. They also block the sun's energy from escaping into space, thereby increasing the earth's temperature. Nature has its own way of maintaining a global equilibrium to ensure life continues on earth. If from human behaviour the earth's temperature rises at an unnatural rate, as it is now doing, the equilibrium ceases to function. Scientists fear this is now happening. As every swimmer knows, water temperatures vary according to the time of the year. They are controlled by the earth's tilt as it revolves round the sun.

While scientists have the technology to calculate the influence on the climate of carbon, methane and ozone as greenhouse gases, they cannot evaluate the influence of water vapour, cloud formation, or wind variations. Perhaps for this reason the Paris Agreement and the IPCC scientists give less attention to the influence of water vapour and clouds on climate change.

As water vapour rises in the atmosphere it cools and precipitates as rain which both cools and warms the earth's atmosphere. But its influence throughout the world is uneven. This is seen in the difference between life in the topics and life in the countries nearer to the Arctic or the Antarctic. The exception is seen in the desert regions of the globe where water vapour is absent and yet temperatures are high.

It is not surprising that scientists, environmentalists and politicians hold different views on these complex issues. We need more scientific research, more public debate and more commitment to act on our findings.

---

8   http://climatechangeconnection.org/references/what-about-water-vapour-reference-list/.

Before examining other factors, human and natural, that determine the prevalence of greenhouse gases, we need to consider the case of the sceptics. Only then can we determine our ongoing course of action.

The Sceptics' Case

The sceptics reject the thesis of the Paris Agreement that the emission of CO_2 is the major factor in the rise of global temperatures, resulting in serious climate change. Sceptics are a minority but they do include some influential scientists, politicians and environmentalists, and they deserve a hearing.

Sceptics reject the fears of politicians such as Jacinda Ardern, the prime minister of New Zealand, who in 2020 claimed that climate change was "a matter of life and death." She stated it was important that all petrol-driven vehicles be replaced by electric ones by 2030.

Sceptics claim that carbon dioxide is a minor gas, with only 3 percent generated by human activity,[9] and that New Zealand's contribution to global emissions is 0.017 percent. They claim almost all CO_2 is produced naturally from the oceans, rocks, volcanoes, and the breath of living creatures. According to the *Washington Post*, the National Oceanic and Atmospheric Administration found that while man-made carbon emissions had declined substantially, atmospheric CO_2 levels continued to rise.[10]

Sceptics do not deny that the increase of greenhouse gases leads to rising temperatures, but they argue that CO_2 is a minor factor. They are also concerned about the action of the "alarmists" to use the present crisis to replace democratic rule with the socialist control of the free market economy. They say alarmists use scaremongering to strengthen government control. Every storm, drought or flood is treated as evidence of climate change and calls for drastic political action. The 2017 *Warning to Humanity: a Second Chance* is an example of this appeal for urgent political action.

Other factors in climate change

I Urban Population Growth

According to the Population Division of the UN Department of Economic and Social Affairs, the world's population is going to increase by 2.5 billion people between 2018 and 2050—in just thirty years' time! This is an

---

[9]   Dr Muriel Newman, *NZ Centre for Political Research* newsletter, 18 June 2021, p. 2.
[10]   Ibid., p. 3.

amazing global growth from the present 7.5 billion people, most of whom live in Asia, Africa and Latin America.

The present 4.2 billion people in urban society will grow to 6.7 billion by 2050. Crucially, 90 percent of these urban dwellers will live in Asia, Africa and Latin America. Cities are expanding. Greater Tokyo has a population of 37 million, New Delhi 29 million, and Shanghai 26 million. Forty-three global cities have at least ten million inhabitants. In these megacities with their large slum populations, there will inevitably be an increase of pollution and rotting garbage which release both carbon and methane into the atmosphere.

If countries in the developed world reached zero carbon increase by 2050, at great economic and social cost, this would not slow the increasing level of carbon in the developing world. It is the cities, not the villages, that are responsible for carbon emissions, and it is the cities that will be needing more fossil fuels as their populations and industries grow. Exxon Mobil plan to increase their production of oil and gas by 25 percent by 2025 to meet the demands of both the developed and the developing world.[11]

As urbanization grows in Asia and Africa, more people are coming into the middle class, with middle class demands. According to the UN Food and Agriculture Organization (FAO) the world will need to produce 70 percent more food by 2050. This will mean more, not fewer, fossil fuels will be needed. Thus, it is unrealistic to think there could be a zero increase in the level of global carbon by 2050.

In view of the likely rise in global temperature, appeals will need to reach the governments of the world to give greater priority to adapting to the present rate of climate change.

2 The Crisis of Deforestation

Deforestation is the destruction of the rainforests and their secondary growth —trees—for industrial and human use and pleasure. It is the global consequence of urban and industrial development. Forests covered more than 30 percent of the earth's surface, but are now under serious threat. Calvin De Witt believes that since 1850, 2.2 billion acres of natural forest have been reclaimed for agricultural and urban use. He estimates this includes an annual loss of 25 million acres of tropical rainforest.[12] The Amazon forests are being cut to provide land for animal grazing, in order to

---

[11]   *The Economist*, 9 February, 2019.
[12]   *The Environment and the Christian*, ed. Calvin De Witt (Grand Rapids, MI, Baker Book House, 1991), pp. 14-17.

provide beef for the American and European markets.[13] It is estimated that 200 square feet of rainforest is needed for each pound of beef. A 5000-kilometre international highway is being built through the Amazon rainforest to meet the need for urban development.

The hardwoods of Asian rainforests from Myanmar to Indonesia—teak, mahogany and others —are being cut, exported and sold to rich families for furniture making and decks for their homes. In many cases the sales are illegal.

Despite the existence of government laws to protect these forests, the logging companies bribe forest officials, politicians and shipping company officials to turn a blind eye to deforestation. Forest fires, some of which have been deliberately started, add to the destruction of the trees.

In Indonesia, the government's law against "slash and burn" is being ignored by contractors. The smoke generated by the burning of the stubble, left when the forest trees are milled, drifts across to Singapore, causing dense smog for up to three months a year. In 2015 smoke from fires in Indonesia contributed to at least 100,000 premature deaths in the region.[14]

Again, since 1977 successive governments of the Solomon Islands have made enormous profits from logging their rainforests. Now, with the forests' serious decline, the national economy has slumped and forest workers are without income.

In Malaysia and Borneo, the forests are being replaced by palm plantations to meet the soaring need for vegetable oil. In comparison to the rainforests, oil palm trees release less oxygen which is needed for all animal and human life.

Another result of deforestation is the serious loss of wildlife—birds, reptiles and mammals. The people who traditionally live in the forests are also losing their natural habitat and are being forced into urban employment.

3 Pollution of the atmosphere

The future of life on the planet depends on clean air. Only then can plant life, especially forests, flourish.

The increasing pollution of the air in the biosphere is endangering life on earth. Mario Neira estimates that two million people die from it every

---

[13] Ibid.
[14] https://www.seas.harvard.edu/news/2016/09/smoke-2015-indonesian-fires-may-have-caused-100000-premature-deaths.

year.[15] Beijing and New Delhi, once clean cities with limited motor traffic, are now among the most polluted cities in the world. China's energy consumption still comes from coal-burning power stations. It had so much pollution that it faced a crisis when the Olympic Games were scheduled for Beijing in August, 2008. For some weeks before the Games, almost all motor traffic was banned from entering the city.

At the same time, China is giving global leadership to the development of the electric car and solar and wind power. Are they doing this for the benefit of the world or for trading purposes?

Human industrial accidents also increase the level of air pollution. One consequence of the Chernobyl disaster on April 20, 1986, was that one-third of the neighbouring state of Belarus became permanently uninhabitable. In Central India, the Union Carbine Company in Bhopal was responsible in 1984 for the tragic leak of methylisocyanate gas, causing the deaths of thousands of people and physical deformities in succeeding generations.

4 The Degradation of the Land

We who live in the early decades of the twenty-first century may not agree on the causes of climate change, or how they relate to one another, but we cannot ignore that it is happening. The degradation of the land is a major factor in this change, and has both natural and human causes. The excessive use of fertilizers and pesticides is poisoning rich farm land. Four areas of degradation are worthy of mention:

Erosion

Because erosion generally happens slowly, the extent of it is underestimated. Ron Sider argued that in the 40 years up to 2010, the earth had lost one-fifth of its topsoil.[16] This may be an exaggeration, but it does point to a serious global problem in the loss of the earth's nutrients. Erosion has two basic causes, one human and the other natural. The earth's surface weathers naturally from the effect of rain, storms and hurricanes. Ice melts, and rushing rivers gouge out the topsoil, carving new channels on plains and hillsides.[17] For example, scientists estimate that the Grand

---

[15]   Mario Neira, "Clean Air, Longer lives," in *The South China Morning Post*, 6 October 2006, A13.

[16]   Tripp, p. 23.

[17]   "Streams, Erosion and Deposition" *in Exercises in Physical Geology*, by W. Kenneth Hamblin and James D. Howard (Upper Saddle River, NJ, Prentice Hall, 1999), p. 95.

Canyon in northern Arizona, a mile-deep gorge, may have been formed five to six million years ago when the Colorado River began to cut a channel through layers of rock.[18] Volcanoes, too, have changed the landscape with their flows of lava and ash.

Moreover, both farmers and logging companies have denuded the hillsides of their vegetation and forests, leading to serious erosion through rain and storms. Erosion is a problem for nations with mountainous regions such as Japan, Nepal and New Zealand. In addition, the overgrazing of cattle and sheep in some hilly areas has resulted in a serious loss of soil.

The misuse of scientific knowledge has further contributed to the loss of topsoil. During the Vietnam War of the early 1970s the use of Agent Orange by the Americans and their allies destroyed vast areas of forest and vegetation. Thus, people have become the chief agents of land degradation, and everybody suffers from it.

Desertification

A second cause of the degradation of the land is the expansion of the deserts. This is seen in the Sahara and the grassy Sahel of North Africa, the Rajasthan desert of north India, and the Gobi desert of northwest China. It is estimated that one-third of the earth's surface is desert.[19] These areas support up to two million people who are finding their region less and less productive. Bruce Bradshaw, a former director of Transformation and Development for World Vision, tells of a farmer in the Sahel region of Africa who lamented that his farm was three times larger than his father's but his harvest was only one-seventh of what his father had harvested forty years before.[20] In the scrubland of the Sahel, the village farmers cut down the remaining bushes for household cooking.

There is some indication, however, that desertification, like climate change, is cyclic. For example, in biblical times, Israel was heavily forested, with plentiful wildlife and abundant water. Then it became largely desert. However, Israelis are now steadily restoring it, with farming and the growing of fruit and vegetables for which they have a global market.

---

[18]   https://www.grandcanyon.org/park-information/canyon-facts/.
[19]   https://www.universetoday.com/65639/what-percentage-of-the-earths-land-sur face-is-desert/.
[20]   Cited in Bruce Nicholls, *Is There Hope for Planet Earth? An ethical response to climate change* (Manila, Asia Theological Association, 2010), p. 6.

Salinization

Where intense heat from the sun evaporates lakes and rivers, such as the Aral Lake in Kazakhstan, salinization increases, making the land less useful. Then through heavy rains and the flooding of rivers, the level of salt may increase in the underground water, especially if that aquifer is near the coast. Under the influence of continuous evaporation, the salt concentration of the aquifer may eventually cause desertification.

5 Water Pollution

A 2010 report by the UN Environmental Program says that more than half of the world's hospital beds are occupied by people suffering from illnesses linked to contaminated water.[21] Women and children from the poor areas are the ones most likely to die from drinking polluted water, and the problem is becoming more serious as the global population increases. Pesticides and fertilizers, and the increasing industrial and now radioactive waste, are polluting the drinking water. Agricultural and animal waste are recognised as other leading causes of contaminated drinking water. Diseases spread by unsafe water include cholera, giardia and typhoid.

As a boy in New Zealand, I enjoyed tramping in the mountain streams in the bush (the New Zealand term for forests.) Giardia, a water-borne dysentery disease, was introduced accidentally by tourists. It is now being spread by possums and it is no longer safe to drink from a mountain stream. In New Zealand the dairy industry is another serious polluter of rivers and lakes. As a result, the government is under pressure to prohibit animals from grazing near the water's edge.

As the world's population grows, more water will be needed for use by households, agriculture, electricity production, industry and transport. Desalinization is being developed in the Middle East and in Singapore, but it is costly. Nations are turning to the underground aquifers but these are being depleted. It is clear that the management of water will be the crisis of the future.

Cities are increasingly dependent on the aquifer. It is estimated that in the USA 40 percent of the people depend on this for their drinking water.[22] In India the overuse of the aquifer to irrigate food crops has resulted in the lowering of the water table. For example, the church in north India that I

---

[21]   Tripp, p. 17.
[22]   https://www.nrdc.org/stories/water-pollution-everything-you-need-know.

pastored found it necessary to deepen its well and lower its water pump by several feet.

As cities expand, many to ten million or more inhabitants, the shortage of clean drinking water becomes critical. New Delhi depends for its drinking water on the Jumna River which flows through it from the Himalayas. Upstream, unrestrained industries in the Punjab pour their toxic waste into the Jumna. With increasing difficulty this water is being purified, but only partially. Tourists to New Delhi often struggle with "Delhi Belly." Those who can afford it drink only bottled water.

The Jumna flows into the equally polluted Ganges at Allahabad, the most sacred location for Hindu religious festivals and for bathing. Many people get sick and die from this polluted water.

The scarcity of drinking water is creating conflict between nations. All the five main rivers of Pakistan have their source in the Himalayas of India. Conflict over the use of this water is always a source of tension between these two nations and could erupt into greater violence.

6 Ocean acidity and pollution

The oceans absorb about 30 percent of carbon dioxide released into the atmosphere. This results in an increased concentration of hydrogen ions in the seawater, causing it to become more acidic, while the carbonate ions cause acidity to decline. These ions are the building blocks of the shells of sea creatures including oysters, sea urchins, corals and plankton.[23] The rain washes pathogens such as bacteria and viruses from the fertilizers, pesticides and animal waste into the rivers and lakes and eventually the oceans, causing a steady rise in the oceans' acidity. Ocean acidification makes it more difficult for marine organisms, such as coral and some plankton, to form their shells and skeletons, and existing shells may begin to dissolve. This acidification also impacts important sectors of the economy such as fisheries and tourism. It affects food supply and makes global warming worse by hindering the oceans' ability to absorb CO_2. For communities that depend on coastal resources, ways of life and cultural identity are threatened.[24]

Adding to the level of acidity is radioactive waste which comes from uranium mining, nuclear plants, the production and testing of military equipment, university experiments and medical research.

---

[23]   https://oceanacidification.noaa.gov/.
[24]   https://www.ucsusa.org/resources/co2-and-ocean-acidification.

7 Plastic Pollution

We all live in a "throwaway culture" with ever-increasing garbage. If it is not regularly treated, this garbage contributes to the level of carbon dioxide. Plastic pollution has become another global issue. The production of plastic is growing faster than its efficient disposal. It has revolutionized medicine and travel by cars and aeroplanes, and supplied bags for household needs and containers for milk. Every year about eight million tons of plastic waste escape into the oceans.[25]

Plastic is made from fossil fuels. In the sunlight and ocean currents, the plastic breaks down into microplastic particles. From there, it cannot be recovered. Seabirds are strangled by microplastics blocking their digestive tracts. Since they can no longer eat properly, they starve to death. Animals as large as elephants also die from consuming plastic. From households to industries, the world has become aware of the plastic crisis, and major efforts are being made to overcome it. But for the present it is one of our most serious environmental challenges.

8 The Loss of Wetlands

Wetlands and peatlands are found in lakes and rivers. Tidal mangroves are a living buffer between land and sea and provide food for many sea creatures fish and birds. They provide a break against tidal waves and tsunamis. They are also crucial to maintaining biodiversity.

Wetlands are a major sink to absorb global carbon dioxide. The world's wetlands are estimated to hold twice as much carbon as all the forests put together. Coastal wetlands can absorb carbon many times faster than the tropical rainforests. So wetlands are a major contributor to limiting the growth of carbon dioxide in the atmosphere and are essential to our sustainable development goals. The tragedy is that 35 percent of all wetlands have been lost since 1970 and at a rate three times greater than the loss of forests.[26] In that period there was an 81 percent decline in inland waterways and a 36 percent decline in coastal and marine species.[27]

---

[25] *National Geographic*, 7 June 2019 https://www.nationalgeographic.com/environ ment/habitats/plastic-pollution/.

[26] Ramsar: Global Wetland Outlook (2018), 5. The Convention on Wetlands of International Importance, more commonly known as the Ramsar Convention, is an international agreement promoting the conservation and wise use of wetlands. Ramsar contributed to the Paris Agreement on Climate Change of 2015.

[27] https://www.environmentguide.org.nz/.

9 The Decline of the Habitat

As a result of the decline of the global habitat, the loss of natural biodiversity is a greater threat to all of life on the earth than is often recognised. Our forests and wetlands, our birds, animals, reptiles and fish are disappearing at a disturbing rate. It is estimated that 70 percent of deforested land has been converted for agricultural use and that half of the world's original forests have disappeared. The rate of deforestation is happening ten times faster than its regrowth. Population growth, urbanization, industrialization, tourism and selfishness are its common causes. In Africa wildlife poaching is leading to a decline in the numbers of elephants and rhinoceroses.

Palm oil plantations have caused the rapid decline of many forests and the food and habitat of many species. This is especially true in Malaysia and Indonesia where their massive palm oil plantations are replacing the rainforests. The WWF's *Living Plantations Report*, released on 10 December 2020, reveals a two-thirds decline in the wildlife population since the 1970s.[28]

Marco Lambertini, Director General of WWF International, says that humanity's increasing destruction of nature is having a catastrophic impact, not only on the wildlife population but also on human health and on all aspects of our lives."[29]

New Zealand illustrates the consequences of exploiting wildlife for its own advancement. Rats, possums, stoats and weasels, originally imported for good reasons, are threatening the natural biodiversity. It is estimated that possums, which may now number about 70 million, consume 21,000 tonnes of green native forest every night.[30] Attempts to eliminate them with 1080 poison have been only partially successful. Rabbits, introduced from Australia, are also consuming the vegetation. It is estimated that since the arrival of the Maori in New Zealand in the thirteenth century, up to 35 percent of all native plants, animals and birds have become extinct.

Sir Ghillean Prance, a tropical rainforest specialist, says "I see about one percent of the remaining forest disappearing every year. Tropical rainforests cover only seven percent of the land surface of the planet, yet they harbour about sixty percent of the species." He then says, "The

---

[28] http://livingplanet.panda.org.
[29] https://www.wwf.org.nz/?17041/WWFs-Living-Planet-2020-Report-reveals-two-thirds-decline-in-wildlife-populations-on-average-since-1970.
[30] http://www.doc.govt.nz:everybodyspossum.pdf.

magnitude of the problem demands ethical, moral and religious solutions, as well as science."[31]

10 Poverty and Social Injustice

Injustice and poverty have a bigger influence on climate change than is often recognised. Where the land is abused, it becomes poorer. Where people lack food and housing, they become diseased and die. Slums increase and garbage is left to rot, producing greenhouse gases. This results in increasing poverty and contributes to climate change.

Social injustice and poverty go hand in hand. When people with limited skills belong to a despised minority, such as the Dalits of India, or to a religion that threatens the exposure of corrupt practices, they lose their jobs, their homes, their possessions and sometimes their lives. To maintain an income, they may become slaves of their employers, as we will see with the Christian brick kiln labourers of Pakistan.

The Millennium Ecosystem Assessment Project of 2005 estimates that one billion people, mainly slum dwellers, survive on less than one dollar per day.

However, most people in the developing world live in villages where they may own a small strip of land or be employed by rich farmers. In times of illness, or to meet culturally demanding obligations such as marriages or funerals, they have to borrow from money lenders who often charge annual interest rates equal to or greater than the amount borrowed. The villagers may then have to sell their cattle on which they depend for their livelihood, and then their land. Finally, they become bondservants or virtual slaves. Tragically, these debts are often passed on to future generations. The result is huge poverty. Those villagers who drift into towns and cities often fail to find employment or a home and become slum dwellers where their poverty is even greater than it was in the village. In desperation they may turn to drugs or gangs, resulting in prison sentences and earlier deaths, often through disease.

Village women may be enticed to the cities with the promise of employment, but then forced into prostitution. Young children become factory or restaurant slaves,

China claims to have lifted a high percentage of its poor out of poverty, but at the cost of its freedom of thought, action and religion. Tragically, the poor of both the developed and the developing nations are becoming

---

[31] *The Care of Creation*, ed. R J Berry (Leicester, Inter-Varsity Press, 2000), p. 115.

poorer, while the rich tend to become richer and more oppressive. Millions of refugees who are fleeing from their homeland are adding to the crisis.

Ultimately, the cause of poverty and injustice is human consumerism and greed. It is people who are abusing the land, cutting down its forests, turning wetlands into farms, draining the aquifer and polluting the air. Change is needed and it must begin with moral transformation.

Chapter 2: Natural Factors in Climate Change

Natural Factors in Climate Change

1 Ice Ages

It is estimated there have been five to six ice ages in the last 600,000 years. Each lasted about 100,000 years, with a warmer and much shorter inter-glacial period between them. The last ice age ended between 11,000 to 8,000 years ago.

During the ice ages the land was covered in ice and sea levels fell up to 100 metres. The ice ages were regional. The last one covered parts of the northern hemisphere, especially Europe, but they were limited in north-east Asia, while in distant New Zealand only the South Island was covered. Forests survived in the North Island. The cause of the ice ages is debated by scientists. There is much support for the Milankovitch Cycle theory which states that each change in the climate is governed by variations in the rotation of the earth around the sun, and that the tilting of the earth's axis determines the difference between summer and winter.

While the level of carbon dioxide has generally been less than 300 ppm, it has varied slightly within each period. It is thought to have been higher during each interglacial period. Some have suggested it was once equal to current levels. How far CO_2 influenced the rise and fall of each ice age is debated. Some scientists have suggested that the level of carbon followed the rise and fall of the global temperatures rather than being the cause of them. Whatever the case, the rise and fall of each ice age was a natural event.

2 The Little Ice Age

Between 1500 and 1700 AD, Europe experienced a Little Ice Age. The river Thames was frozen eleven inches thick. In London shops and stalls were built on the ice covering the Thames, and horse and coach races were held. Since then the climate has varied considerably.

At present we are in a warm period following the last ice age, but some scientists see signs that the earth is beginning to cool again. We have seen that global temperatures are not constant. They again decreased between

1950 and 1980 and have been gradually increasing since 1985. In 1952 I delivered Christmas mail in London in the midst of snow and ice. Now London has little or no snow at Christmas.

As already mentioned, since the mid-nineteenth century the earth's surface temperature has risen by 1 degree Celsius, but most of this increase came after 1975. The scientific consensus, as summarized by the IPCC in 2007, was: "Most of the observable increase in global average temperatures since the mid-20th century is most likely due to the observed increase in anthropogenic greenhouse gas concentrations."[32]

Perhaps it is too early to predict what the temperature of the earth will be in 2050, and certainly we could not do so by the end of 2021. We could have another cool period before then, or the temperature could rise naturally by 2 degrees C. A drastic contraction of the economy, including agriculture, in order to reach a zero carbon increase by 2050, may not be possible. Certainly, few countries in the developing world would be willing to make the sacrifices necessary to achieve this.

New Zealand is an example of a country that is taking drastic action to reduce the carbon increase by 2050. However, the farming community, with urban support, is vigorously opposing this effort. It has been pointed out that if the global carbon dropped to 160 ppm, all life on earth would die. Productivity depends on the availability of adequate carbon. As we mentioned in Chapter One, the rising level of carbon has benefited the greening of the earth.

The density of the greenhouse shield that surrounds the earth increases the retention of solar energy on the earth's surface, thereby raising the level of global temperatures. The IPCC scientists are right to recognise the influence of the combined greenhouse gases on the rise in global temperatures. But the debate continues on how *influential* the level of carbon in the greenhouse gases is. Is it a major or minor influence compared to other gases in the greenhouse shield, including water vapour which results in more clouds and winds and changing ocean currents? All of them cool the earth's surface.

So the composition of the greenhouse gases is the major divide between the "alarmists" and the "sceptics." We affirm that the more this issue is debated, the more likely we are to understand the composition of GHGs and their influence on the global climate.

It is disappointing that the IPCC scientists show little enthusiasm to debate these issues with those who do not accept their findings. It is also

---

[32]   Cited Tapio Schneider, "How We Know Global Warming is Real," Sceptic Magazine, 1/21, 2019, p. 2.

unfortunate that little of the available funding is shared with those who hold alternative views to the IPCC. Moreover, the media get more traction from reporting the alarmist view than the sceptical one.

The present climatic disturbances are clearly increasing in severity. But even if zero carbon increase were to be achieved by 2050 it might take several decades to restore the climatic equilibrium. Governments must be prepared for a slow recovery. Relief agencies can play a part in restoring the climate balance as they reduce poverty and promote sustainable development.

The comment of Dr Sam Solanki, director of the Max Planck Institute for Solar Systems Research in Göttingen, Germany, is pertinent:

"A brighter sun and higher levels of greenhouse gases such as carbon dioxide have both contributed to a change in the earth's temperature, and it is impossible to say which has the greater impact."[33]

3 Volcanic Activity

While volcanic activity is not caused by humans, its influence on human lives and on the environment can be significant. It is generally agreed that its impact on climate change is small since the climatic effect of each explosion lasts only two or three years. But the cumulative effect of several eruptions and earthquakes over a short period can make a difference to the climate.

For example, since 1991 there has been a number of large eruptions across Asia. Since 2013 there have been a series of volcanic explosions around the "Ring of Fire." This is a horseshoe-shaped belt of earthquake and volcanic eruptions around the Pacific Ocean, stretching from South America to the west coast of the USA, down to Japan, the Philippines, Indonesia, Papua New Guinea and the Pacific Islands to New Zealand. Of the 141 volcanic explosions across Asia, there have been five major ones since 2010. These are:

Mt Agung in Bali, Indonesia, in November 2017; Sinabung in Sumatra, Indonesia, in August 2010; and eruptions in the Philippines, Papua New Guinea, and Japan in January 2018. These volcanoes emitted millions of tonnes of carbon dioxide (CO_2) and sulphur dioxide (SO_2) into the air, along with large flows of molten rock, lava and mud. Millions of people who lived within ten kilometres of these major eruptions were severely affected. Then the release of polluting gases through volcanic activity in the depths

---

[33] Dr Sam Solanki, *Sunday Times*, July 18, 2004.

of the ocean has also added to the level of air pollution and has probably had a greater influence on the climate than land explosions.

Tsunamis sometimes follow volcanic activity. Tsunamis in Japan have destroyed whole towns, with a large loss of life. For example, in Indonesia on 26 December, 2004, a massive tsunami in Aceh, caused by an ocean rupture along the fault between the Burma Plate and the Indian Plate, killed more than 200,000 people in fourteen Asian countries. The so-called Sendai tsunami, off the northeast coast of the Tōhoku region of Japan's Honshu Island, occurred on March 11, 2011. Its wall of water 38 metres high killed more than 20,000 people.

Volcanoes, both on land and under the sea, release large amounts of gases and heat which contribute to the warming of the atmosphere. At the same time, they create dense clouds which cool the earth's temperature. When Mount Pinatubo erupted in Luzon, the Philippines, on June 15, 1991, it was the second-largest volcanic eruption of the 20th century, behind only the 1912 eruption of Novarupta in Alaska.[34] This Luzon eruption blasted into the air an estimated 20 million tons of sulphur dioxide, reduced the amount of solar radiation reaching the earth's surface, and covered a large area with ash. There was widespread destruction and loss of life. However, like all eruptions, its impact on climate change was short-lived, only two or three years.

Signs of Hope

I Reduction in the Use of Fossil Fuels

During the coronavirus lockdowns, the global use of fossil fuels radically dropped. This was evident in at least six sectors of the economy, namely the electric power industry, surface road and sea transport, aviation, residential heating, and heating in public buildings. The real test will be after the decline of the coronavirus, to know whether the decreased dependence on fossil fuels can be sustained.

As we have noted, New Zealand is one western country that is making major progress in reducing the level of carbon. On the recommendations of the Climate Change Commission, the government is implementing a number of carbon reduction strategies, including that all new cars must be electric by 2030; cycling and walking lanes are to be doubled; the use of public transport is to increase; and farmers are to reduce the emissions of methane gas. The remaining coal and gas plants must be phased out; and

---

[34]   https://en.wikipedia.org/wiki/1991_eruption_of_Mount_Pinatubo.

forests of pine will be replaced by native trees. The question is, will the public accept such drastic sacrifices? The following national election will decide. New Zealand's contribution to reducing carbon is miniscule, but the government sees its policies as a model for global action. The developed world has begun to accept restrictions on the use of fossil fuels, while the developing world is bent on raising its standard of living and thus *increasing* its need for more fossil fuels.

2 Reforestation and Afforestation

Reforestation and afforestation are two related ways of restoring the forests' ecosystems. Reforestation is replanting trees native to the region in areas where deforestation has depleted them. It is rebuilding natural habitats and ecosystems. Green vegetation through photosynthesis absorbs carbon dioxide. It is a main carbon sink, saving the world from environmental disaster. Sustainable development in many countries depends on reforestation as an important way to reduce climate change. Asia, China and India are making commendable efforts to increase tree planting. In China, forest coverage has increased by 16 percent since 1970. In some provinces all high school students are required to plant one tree per year.

In the state of Uttar Pradesh, India, 50 million trees were planted in 2016. The state of Madhya Pradesh planted 66 million trees in 2017. Since 1948, Israel has planted 240 million trees.[35] The 2020 World Economic Forum at Davos created the "Trillion Tree" campaign with the aim of planting one trillion trees across the globe.[36]

Afforestation is establishing a forest in an environment where there are no trees. It is part of the sustainable policy of many governments and nongovernmental agencies worldwide. It is not as successful as reforestation, where the soil is naturally better prepared for native seedlings

All trees and plants absorb carbon dioxide through photosynthesis, and forests are examples of carbon sinks which store large amounts of carbon. One estimate is that forests remove about 3 billion tons of carbon per year from the atmosphere, which is about 30 percent of all carbon emissions.[37] Clouds produce rain, and together they lower the earth's temperatures. So the renewing of the world's forests is a natural way to reduce climate change.

---

[35] https://en.wikipedia.org/wiki/reforestation.
[36] Ibid.
[37] Valentine Bettassen, *Carbon Sequestration*, hpps://www.nature.com/news/carbon-sequestration (13.2.2014).

3 Miniature Forests in Cities—the Miyaki way

Expanding cities are increasing global pollution which leads to the deaths of millions each year. Their concrete buildings and tarmac roads absorb the sun's rays rather than reflecting them back into space, thereby generating more heat. As the megacities of Asia grow, these twin evils of pollution and increased carbon are becoming increasingly evident, adding to the crisis of climate change.

Dr Miyaki Akira, formerly of Yokohama University in Japan, has developed a method of growing miniature forests within cities.[38] Instead of planting trees in rows, as in reforestation, he follows nature's way of promoting forest growth. He analyses the soil of empty spaces in cities and if necessary, fertilizes it with natural manures. He then scatters a wide range of seeds of trees, shrubs and ground-covering herbs, as found in the native forest, and distributes them with high intensity. As they grow, they struggle for sunlight. This forces them to grow faster. For three years the "constant gardener" as he calls himself, waters them and then leaves them to fend for themselves. Within ten to twenty years the site has become a miniature forest within the city, creating a carbon sink and thereby reducing pollution but also cooling the rising urban temperatures.

As example of the Miyaki method, these inner-city miniature forests are being developed in many cities in Japan and now across Asia, especially in the megacities of India. This method is also becoming popular across several cities in Europe and Latin America and supplements the work of reforestation and afforestation. The restoring of forests may become a more effective way of reducing climate change.

4 Recovery of the Ozone Layer

The hole in the ozone layer, principally over the Antarctic and southern hemisphere, every August to October, was discovered by a British Antarctic survey in the 1970s. The ozone layer, which is 15-30 km up in the stratosphere, protects life on earth from the harmful ultraviolet radiation from the sun. In 1970s scientists in the British Antarctic survey discovered that chlorofluorocarbons (CFCs) were a serious threat to the ozone layer, and that the level of ozone over the Antarctic was dropping at an astonishing rate from August to October each year, endangering the health of people and animals in the southern hemisphere.

---

[38]   "The Constant Gardener," *The Economist*, 3 July 2021, p. 676-68.

The effect of this hole has been an increase in cataracts and fatal cancers in Australia and New Zealand. In 1987 the Montreal Protocol required countries to phase out the use of chlorofluorocarbons (CFCs) in refrigerators and air conditioners. It was signed by 187 nations. It was enacted in 1989 and has been successful, largely because it represented united action between scientists and governments. In January 2019 it was strengthened by the Kigali Amendment designed to enforce the law against the use of CFCs. The ozone layer is now recovering by 1 percent to 3 percent per decade. A complete recovery in the northern hemisphere is expected by 2030, in the southern hemisphere by 2050, and in the Antarctic by 2060.[39]

This action gives hope that human beings can recover from their environmental mistakes and shortcomings.

5 Poverty in Decline

A sustainable society will not be reached without reducing the level of worldwide poverty. Poverty means poor housing, a lack or absence of sanitation, unemployment, and above all a lack of food and clean drinking water. For many African and Asian nations, poverty is defined as an income of less than the equivalent of $US1.75 per day.

While the level of poverty has been reduced in several countries (in Africa it has declined by an average of 10 percent over the last thirty years), the number of poor is increasing as national populations rise. Urban slums are pockets of poverty and unemployment, although rural populations are generally poorer than urban ones.

China has had the greatest success in reducing poverty. According to a World Bank report, 850 million people in China, mainly urban ones, have been lifted out of extreme poverty. The World Bank sets the poverty level at $5.50 a day and states China is now an upper-middle-income country according to this metric. However, about a quarter of China's population remain in poverty with an income of less than $5.50 per day and there is widespread income inequality. Last year, Chinese Premier Li Keqiang said China still had 600 million people whose monthly income was barely 1,000 yuan ($154)—not enough to rent a room in a city. Nevertheless, over the last few decades, China has made huge strides to lift millions out of the toughest standards of living.[40]

India has also made progress as salaries increase and rural people are better able to diversify their income. As of 2020, its incidence of

[39]   https//believe.earth/en/recovery-of-the-ozone-layer-brings-hope/.
[40]   https://www.bbc.com/news/56213271.

multidimensional poverty has significantly reduced from 54.7 percent in 2005 to 27.9 percent in 2015-16. According to the United Nations Development Programme Administrator Achim Steiner, India lifted 271 million people out of extreme poverty in a ten-year period from 2005/06 to 2015/16.[41]

We have explored both the human and the natural causes of climate change, but the relationship between them will continue to be debated for years to come.

[41]   https://en.wikipedia.org/wiki/Poverty_in_India.

Chapter 3: A Biblical Understanding of Creation Care

The first chapter of Genesis is about God's progressive creation of the earth. It is about the one true Creator God whose existence is beyond definition by logic or science. The challenge is to believe and trust in the God who revealed himself symbolically in seven days of creation. Stephen Hawking claimed that the theories of relativity and quantum physics explained the origin of the universe. This is neither true nor possible.[42] Science is not the creator of life; God is. Moreover, he who created all things has entrusted the care of creation to us and he will hold us accountable for the way we live and use it.

The unity of God's progressive creation

The story of creation in Genesis 1 is about God bringing light out of darkness, order out of chaos, and purpose out of confused identity. Science focuses on the how of creation, while the biblical record focuses on its meaning and purpose.

The proper response to the creation story is to believe in the creator God and to trust and obey him. As a doubting university student, I had as my anchor Hebrews 11:6 which states that "without faith it is impossible to please God, because anyone who comes to him must believe that he exists and that he rewards those who earnestly seek him."

Contrary to secular humanism and the traditional faiths of Asia, the biblical record asserts that God created the time/space universe out of nothing (*creatio ex nihilo*) by the command of his eternal Word. Ten times in the first chapter of Genesis we read "God said," and it happened. His command, "Let there be ..." occurs eight times. Islam has a similar understanding of God's creative act. He said "Be!" and it happened (Surah 3:59). The word "day" is a symbol for a period of unstated length. The days in creation are relative to each other; not literally 24 hours each.

Moreover, God delights in his creation. After each day of creation, it states that "God saw that it was good." It satisfied his purpose. Then on the sixth day, when he created the animals and human beings, he breathed the "breath of life" into them both and said, "It is very good." We share similar

---

42   David Wilkinson, *The Message of Creation* (Leicester: Inter Varsity Press, 2002), pp. 22-23.

physiology, but spiritually human beings are unique. We are each created in the image and likeness of God, male and female, and he gave us the responsibility to rule over the whole of creation and to care for it (Genesis 2:15). The tragedy is that human beings have not lived up to God's expectations to care for the earth. We have destroyed the primal forests, polluted the air, land and sea, and become agents of abuse and death. Advocates of reducing the effect of the increasing carbon in the air need to recognise that saving the planet begins not with politics and science but with faith in the One whom Jews, Christians and Muslims recognise as the Creator of all things.

As human beings we marvel at the creation of non-human life, as seen in the continuity of plants, birds, fish and animals, each reproducing according to its own kind, as repeated in Genesis 1:11-12, 22, 24, 25. I am amazed at how the smallest insect, flower and bird instinctively reproduces "after its own kind." This is beyond our comprehension. It is not an aimless evolution or the survival of the fittest, but the way of a loving, purposeful, creative God, who cares for the most insignificant of his creatures.

It is amazing how the whole of creation, with its countless distinctives, exists in harmony, each part dependent on the other. The contemplation of nature is an invitation to wonder[43] at the teeming complexity of life and the enormous power in the atom. Our task is to develop a biblical theology of nature and to give thanks. But faith seeks understanding, and that is the purpose of this chapter.

Faith begins with meditating on the majesty of God (Psalm 8). The first three days of creation deal with its shape, and the second three days with filling in that shape. God is the great Artist. He is an extravagant God who delights in creativity and diversity.[44]

The crown of creation

People share with animals the same breath of life, *nephesh* (Genesis 2:7). They were both created on the sixth day and share the same DNA. They are dependent on each other, yet there is a fundamental difference between them. God said, "Let us make humankind (Adam) in our own image and likeness" (Genesis 1:26). So God created Adam and Eve as the

---

[43]   Robert P Meye, "Invitation to Wonder: Towards a Theology of Nature" in *Tending the Garden*, ed. Wesley Granberg-Michaelson (Grand Rapids, MI, Eerdmans, 1990), p. 30.

[44]   David Wilkinson, *The Message of Creation* (BST) (Leicester, Inter-Varsity Press, 2002), p. 24-25.

progenitors of the whole human race which was to live together as families in community. I identify with those scholars who believe that Adam and Eve were historical persons, the founders of the distinctly human race. Both Jesus and Paul affirmed this identity. Paul called Jesus the "second Adam." (Romans 5:12-14). Adam and Eve's relationship to any subhuman beings that may have existed before them on the earth, such as the Neanderthals, is not clear.

Adam as the representative of humankind is the source of all humanity. He is the federal head of all his descendants, so that when Adam sinned, we all identified with him in our sin. The good news is that by faith in Christ we also share in his death and resurrection, and in the assurance of eternal life, for as Saviour he is the head of all who commit their lives to him.

God created humankind in his own image and likeness with the capacity to use language and to relate personally and rationally to himself. The animal kingdom has remained the same through the centuries, while the human race has progressed in its knowledge of the created world, as we see in science and technology today. Our ability to relate to God has, however, remained the same. Abraham, who lived about 4000 years ago, had a living relationship with God, no less than we have today.

A unique element in this divine-human relationship is the gift of conscience, an innate knowledge of right and wrong. Paul makes frequent reference to this in his letters. One of the consequences of being sinful is that our consciences can be misused, abused or ignored. Only a continuing relationship with God himself can purify our hearts and give us good consciences. Jesus said, "Blessed are the pure in heart, for they will see God" (Matthew 5:8).

Paul says that all people have a knowledge of God's "eternal power and divine nature" but also that they suppress the truth by their wickedness (Romans 1:18-20).

The complementary nature of God's revelation

God, the Creator and Redeemer of all things, reveals himself in word and deed. The Psalmist contemplated God's glory when he said, "The heavens declare the glory of God; the skies proclaim the work of his hands" (Psalm 19:1). He then added, "Day and night display his speech and knowledge" (vv 2-3).

People of every culture experience awe at creation, but sadly not all of them know God's personal name or the way of salvation which has been revealed in the Scriptures, first to Jews and then to Christians. That is, most people have only general or universal revelation.

It is only in the revelation of Jesus Christ that the seeker can find peace with the living God who has revealed himself as the Saviour of the world. This salvation is announced uniquely in the Bible. We call this *special* revelation, as distinct from *general* revelation,

Our evangelistic task is to build bridges between people who are seekers of the gods they know, and Jesus Christ, as recorded in the Gospels. Our prayer is that these seekers will discover for themselves who Christ is and why he died and rose again, and that faith in him brings eternal life.

Stewards of Creation

The Psalms are noted for their wonder at the goodness of God in all his creative acts. By his Spirit he renews creation and the face of the earth (Psalm 104:30).

God is the sovereign King over all he has created, the plants the fish, the animals, and human beings. It is an awesome responsibility for us to be his stewards over everything he has made.

God blessed the first couple and told them to multiply, to fill the earth with their descendants and to subdue it (v28). They were to rule or have dominion over all living beings. The words "have dominion" and "subdue" are strong because God foresaw that the challenges they would face would demand firm action. The further use of "to have dominion," which is quoted 23 times in the Old Testament, shows its importance. The word "to subdue" was regularly used of the land they were to occupy although not without a struggle. The history of Israel under Joshua, the judges and the kings gives evidence of this responsibility of stewardship.

Moses promised God's chosen people that if they faithfully obeyed God's commands, he would set them above all the nations[45] but if they failed in their stewardship, they would be punished and the whole of creation would suffer with them. Hosea had the same message: if Israel were unfaithful to the Lord, they would be cursed and the land would mourn (Hosea 4:1-3).

Philip Church summarizes the much-debated words "have dominion over" and "subdue" as: "Humans are co-creators with God, continuing the

---

[45]   Deuteronomy 28:1-4.

work of creation, and ordering the world to support plant and animal life as it fruitfully multiplied."[46]

When Adam and Eve rebelled against God's rule, God punished them and the whole creation. He cursed the serpent, he increased women's pain in childbirth, and he cursed the ground so that it was cultivated only through painful toil, "through the sweat of Adam's brow."

Dominion not domination

Much has been written in response to Lynn White's article, "The Historical Roots of our Ecological Crisis," first published in 1967, in which he accused Christians of using Genesis 1:26-28 to justify their domination and destruction of creation. He concluded by saying, "Hence we will continue to have a worsening ecological crisis until we reject the Christian axiom that nature has no reason for existence save to serve man."[47]

While it is sometimes true that Christians have dominated nature for selfish reasons rather than serving it in the biblical spirit of having dominion, the accusation misunderstands the intent of these two concepts which are sometimes conflated.

A modern example of dominion becoming domination is seen in the present misuse of biotechnology in genetic engineering which could endanger the health of future generations. Modified genes once altered cannot be restored to their original condition. There is also the danger of introducing toxic genes.

The destruction of the primal forests in order to grow palm trees for their oil is yet another example of human "domination" of nature, motivated by greed and selfishness.

From Abraham to John the Baptist

During the 2000 years between Abraham and John the Baptist, the last prophet, the covenant relationship between God and his people oscillated between fruitful obedience and disastrous disobedience leading to national fragmentation. This was seen early on, in the people's building the Tower of Babel in order to make a name for their posterity. However, God

---

[46]   Philip Church, "What Are Human Beings that You are Mindful of them?" (Hebrews 2:5) in the book, *Creation and Hope*, eds. Nicola Hoggard Creegan and Andrew Shepherd (Eugene, OR: Pickwick, 2018), p. 128.

[47]   Lynn White, "The Historical Roots of the Ecological Crisis" published in *Science* 155:1203-1207. It is reprinted in full in *The Care of Creation*, ed. R J Berry (pp. 31-42).

confused their language and scattered them over the face of the earth. (Genesis 11:1-9).

God then chose Abraham from the pagan city of Ur of the Chaldeans, blessed him and made a covenant with him with two promises. One was that his descendants would multiply and that all people on the earth would be blessed through him (Genesis 12:2-3). This has proved true. Nations have been blessed through the contribution of Jews in their midst. The second promise was the gift of the land of Canaan as an everlasting possession (Genesis 17:8).

The history of this long period saw obedience with blessing alternating with failure and suffering. This pattern of response was seen with Moses and the people during the wilderness journey and it continued under Joshua and the Judges. God blessed Moses by making a covenant with him and giving him ten laws on Mount Sinai. Sadly, in Moses' brief absence from the community, the people turned against Yahweh and worshipped a golden calf as a fertility god. God immediately punished them with a plague (Exodus 32:1-35).

The same pattern continued through the reign of the kings down to the exile in Babylon. The irony is that during the following 70 years of exile, the land of Israel enjoyed a sabbatical rest (2 Chronicles 36:21). During this time the land was being restored to its fruitfulness.

The restoration of the land to the Israelites under Ezra and Nehemiah during the reign of the Persian kings was followed by 480 years of political confusion up to the coming of John the Baptist, the forerunner of Jesus, the promised Messiah,

Throughout this period, the land was a defining issue. God's relationship with Israel was an unconditional one of "I will be your God and you shall be my people" (Genesis 17:17, Exodus 6:7). However, the promise of the land was also conditional, based on the people's faithfulness to the covenant.

The Promised Land and the city of Jerusalem have since oscillated between possession and loss. First, in the time of Christ, the land was under occupation by the Romans. From the seventh century AD until the British mandate of 1917, it was under Muslim control. The tragic crusades of the eleventh to the thirteenth centuries never permanently liberated Jerusalem from its enemies.

The present division of the land between Israel and the West Bank (known as Palestine) has no political solution. Ultimately, Israel will never agree to a two-state division as promoted by the United Nations. The conflict between Israel and the Muslim nations could erupt at any time into a global conflict, but the future is in the hands of God who will not deny his covenantal promises.

From the First Covenant to the New Covenant

The history of Israel from Moses to the Exile, and the return of the remnant to Jerusalem, is the story of God keeping his covenant relationship with his chosen people. It was a time of blessing when they were faithful to their covenant promises, and a time of punishment when they were not. The compassion and love of God is seen in his offer to make a new covenant with his people after they had failed to keep the first one. It reveals him as a longsuffering God who would make a new covenant at great personal cost when he redeemed his people at the cross.

God chose an insignificant Jew, Moses, arranged his education in the house of Pharaoh, taught him lessons of dependence in the desert, and gave him courage to lead his people out of Egypt. The Exodus was the work of God's saving grace and was constantly in the minds of the Israeli people throughout their history. It continues to be the centre of the Jewish faith. Moses was called to make known the will of God through "Ten Words" given to him in a unique mountaintop experience. They were followed by many religious, social and political laws, recorded in the Pentateuch, given to guide the nation in holiness.

Moses' lengthy farewell address to the people tells of God's love for all of creation and it tells of God's justice in punishing the people when they fail to keep their promises. He ends his farewell with "The Eternal God is your refuge, and underneath are the everlasting arms ... blessed are you O Israel! Who is like you, a people saved by the LORD?" (Deuteronomy 33: 27, 29).

After Moses there was a period of turmoil under the judges, until God raised up David, the eighth son of Jesse. The prophet Isaiah recalls vividly how the Spirit of the Lord rested on David and gave him a spirit of wisdom, understanding, counsel and power.

To Isaiah God gave the unique gift of prophesying the day when whole of creation would be renewed. In this prophecy the animals would be at peace with themselves and with humanity (Isaiah 11:1-16). Isaiah takes up this hope in terms of God creating a new heaven and new earth which would be a time of universal blessing (Isaiah 65:17-25). But it was left to Jeremiah to give details of the new covenant relationship in which God said "I will put my law in their minds and write it on their hearts. I will be their God and they will be my people" (Jeremiah 31:33). He then promised to forgive their wickedness and remember their sins no more (v34).

Then followed the Exile and Daniel and Ezekiel's messages to those in bondage, first in Assyria and then in Babylon. God promised to renew those returning to Jerusalem, where their fields would yield abundant crops and the people would be secure in their land. The Valley of Dry Bones would be restored to life (Ezekiel 37:1-14).

Jesus and Creation

It is clear from the gospels that Jesus had a strong sense of identity with God his Father, with the world of nature and with his Hebrew culture. We can assume he worked in the carpenter's shop with Joseph until he began his public ministry at about 30 years of age. He began by preaching that "The time has come, the kingdom of God is near. Repent and believe the good news" (Mark 1:15). He repeated this message of the kingdom to all his contacts.

He went on to demonstrate this message by healing the sick and the diseased, feeding the hungry, and liberating people from bondage to evil spirits. He identified with people in their poverty and vigorously opposed Satan and the world of demonic power. His first miracle was turning water into wine, symbolising his identity with the land. One of his last miracles was to restore the ear of the servant of the high priest at the moment of his arrest. He was compassionate to all in need and spoke firmly against injustice wherever he found it, as with the money changers in the temple (Matthew 21:12-13 and Luke 19 :45-46).

Jesus identified with his Jewish culture and with the Hebrew worship in the synagogues and temple. A major part of his ministry was the healing of the sick and the exorcism of evil spirits. He clearly distinguished between them, as seen in Matthew 4:23-25 and Matthew 9:27-34. The demonic power of Satan and his evil spirits was directed against Jesus from the time of his wilderness experience, so that exorcism became a central part of his ministry.

Then Jesus passed this power onto his disciples (Matthew 10:1-10). Exorcism is still important in evangelism, especially among people in Hindu, Buddhist and Islamic cultures.

As we have seen, Jesus lived close to nature. He pointed to the ways God cared for his creation—the birds of the air, the lilies of the field (Matthew 6:21-34) and the life of the common sparrow. He even knew the number of hairs on his disciples' heads (Matthew 10:29-30). From nature Jesus taught the coming of the kingdom in power and in blessing. Matthew 13 lists seven of his parables illustrating the message of the kingdom. These included the sower and the seeds, the weeds and the good seeds growing together, the explosive growth of the mustard seed from the tiniest seed to the largest tree, the impact of leaven on dough to make bread, the hidden treasure in the field, the pearl of great price, and the net which caught an abundance of fish. In each case we see Jesus' love and respect for nature.

In his first sermon in the synagogue at Nazareth, Jesus explained from the prophecy of Isaiah that the Spirit of the Lord was upon him to liberate the poor, the prisoner, the blind and the oppressed, and to announce the promise of the coming Jubilee year of the restoration of the land to its owners (Isaiah 61:1-2). Jesus applied this passage to his own commission in Luke 4:18-19. Hans Küng summarized Jesus' ministry as "God's kingdom is creation healed."[48] This phrase brings together the divine and the physical in his ministry.

Again and again, Scripture shows humanity suffering from poverty, disease and war, and creation groaning from its abuse. Jesus came as a suffering Messiah to redeem humanity. When he suffered on the cross, God suffered. When he rose in triumph from the dead, God triumphed with him. Jesus' "seven words from the Cross" record his forgiveness, and his care for others. He was aware that his dying was an atonement for the sins of the people. In his resurrection body the realms of divine and human came together. The amazing fact is that in his ascension he took his physical humanity into eternity so that heaven and earth became one in that momentous event which foreshadowed the resurrection of the believer.

The letters of Paul on Creation

Paul in Colossians 1:15-20 gives a profound insight into Jesus' relationship with God and the cosmos. From prose he bursts into poetry to express the language of both mind and heart. He says Jesus is the image of the invisible and eternal God, the creator of all things. He is the source of the healing of all creation. In him all things hold together.

Many scientists believe the universe began with a "big bang," a view of the beginning that is consistent with this biblical revelation. However, they also believe it will eventually implode on itself, whereas the Bible points to the renewal or re-creation of the earth. The universe's enormous power is seen in the world of the atom. In Colossians Paul says Christ is the source of the power holding the universe together. All the fullness of God is in him. He alone will restore the earth to its original pre-human grandeur by reconciling all things to himself through his suffering on the cross. We look forward to the restoration of the Garden of Eden.

---

[48]   Hans Küng, *On Being a Christian* (Glasgow: Collins, 1978) p. 231.

In another defining passage (Romans 8:18-27) already discussed in the Introduction, Paul states that creation is "groaning" and that Christ and his Spirit will liberate it from its bondage to decay and groaning into glorious freedom. But, says Paul, the children of God are also groaning from their sin and are awaiting their adoption as his sons and daughters. Paul continues his good news "that all things work together for good to those who love God ..." and that "we are more than conquerors through him who loved us" (Romans 8:28, 37).

While Paul emphases salvation as justification by faith alone, when talking to the legalists, then and now, his emphasis on salvation as reconciliation has a strong appeal to Asians with their longing for inner peace and harmony and with people's integration with nature.

Paul says anyone who is in Christ is a new creation (2 Corinthians 5:11-21). He again stresses in his message to the Colossian church that God is reconciling all things to himself. This is made possible through the death of Jesus on the cross (Colossians 1:15-23). Paul would respond to the fear of climate change with the plea for unbelievers to return to their Creator who alone can save the earth from human destruction and restore it to its original goodness.

Many believe the current climate crises are cyclical, being of both short and long duration and that their effects are felt differently in different parts of the earth. The ultimate hope for the earth is beyond the limits of science and technology. It will depend on people being willing to change their lifestyles. In conversion to Christ, many people become willing to live more simply and to be God's agents in the restoration of creation. Local churches are called to accept their responsibility to be stewards of creation and to be willing to make changes to be agents of its liberation, recognising that it is God alone who will redeem it. This is our Christian hope.

Longing for life beyond death

The people of the world long for life beyond death. They long for liberation from the human suffering which is so evident in the world today. Each religion is concerned with the final end of life—death. They have wondered from generation to generation, Is there life after death? Will it be good or evil? Many people have become secular in a materialistic and consumerist world and find no meaning in the concept of life beyond death. They live only for the pleasures that the material world offers and believe that death will end their existence.

Hindus strive to live moral lives according to the law of karma, so that in the next life their status will be raised, with the eventual hope of moksha as freedom from the continuing cycle of life and death.

Buddhists long for a nirvana of peace and the end of all suffering. They strive to find it by living according to the Eightfold Path, or in the case of Mahayana Buddhists, by following the Pure Land or Zen Buddhist beliefs. They look for union with a cosmic Buddha. The idea of eternal life horrifies Buddhists, for they are looking for an end to the cycle of rebirths.

To evangelize Hindus and Buddhists we must relate to them from their own cultural values before we can lead them to Jesus in the Gospels as the fulfilment of their eternal hope.[49]

Muslims devote their lives to prayer and the keeping of sharia law, in the hope that Allah will be merciful to them on the Day of Judgment and release them to paradise where they will enjoy the pleasures they have failed to achieve in this life. In evangelizing Muslims, we need to follow a similar procedure of relating to their cultural values, beginning with Isa (Jesus) in the Qur'an and then to Jesus in the Gospels.

Jews and *Christians* have a strong belief that death is not the end, and that heaven, not hell, is their destination. Christians who live by the truth of the whole Bible and trust in Jesus as their Lord and Saviour are confident of eternal life with Jesus in his kingdom. Our acceptance of the resurrection of Jesus becomes the basis for belief in our own resurrection to eternal life. In the resurrection of Jesus, we see the transformation to a life which is no longer limited by time and space. This was made possible by the cross. The Greek concept of immortality is replaced by the biblical concept of eternal life for all who trust in Jesus. The bodily resurrection of Jesus to his Father suggests that heaven is both a place and a relational state and that the earth will be transformed into the new earth of Christ's kingdom. Will this renewed earth become our heaven? I think so.

As disciples of Jesus, we are responsible for the care of creation from now to the Day of Judgment when we give an account of our stewardship of it. May we be found faithful.

---

[49] See Bruce Nicholls, *Building Bridges from Asian Faiths to Jesus in the Gospels* (Oxford, Regnum Publishers, 2019). For a discussion on introducing Muslims to Isa (Jesus) in the Qur'an and in the Gospels. See pp. 132-133.

Chapter 4: A Theology of the Cosmos

The much-loved verse, John 3:16, begins with *hotos*, translated "so," indicating the extent of God's love. "For God so loved the world that he gave ..."

God's love for our cosmos, or world, was so great that he gave himself in the person of his only Son, to redeem it. In the rest of chapter three John talks about the salvation of the human race as those who have come to the Light (v20) and have believed in the Son to receive eternal life. The message of the cross, the resurrection and the ascension of Christ points to his saving love, involving both the physical and the spiritual world. For in the ascension, Christ took humanity with him into the Father's eternal presence.

This past week I was listening to a CD of Stainer's *The Crucifixion*. When it came to the baritone singing "God so loved the world that he gave ..." I was deeply moved by the extent of God's love, its purpose and its cost. I was immediately drawn to John chapter one, where the writer speaks of the light shining in the darkness and the darkness not overcoming it (v5). I read again of God's love for the world, as recorded in Genesis chapter one, where God overcame the darkness of the formless void and step by step created the world, culminating with animals and human beings on Day Six. Thus, in John 3:16 we are introduced to God's deep love for the cosmos.

Stephen Pattemore of the South Pacific Bible Society argues that the cosmos in John 3:16, if taken in the context of John chapter one, includes God's love for all creation, nature and human beings. God saw that all he created was "very good," meaning he was satisfied with all of it. Pattemore adds that we need to be seized with a passion for "our common home."[50] I prefer to call this "our shared home," for we—animals and human beings—are dependent on one another and on nature. Without the breathing of the green forests and plants we would all die, and without our breathing they would all die. Our animal pets have learned to accept a common home with us and we must learn to share our common home with them.

The fourth Mosaic law states we are to share a day of rest with our working animals. This shared home is seen in the extent of the Sabbath Year where the land was to be left fallow for one year in seven (Leviticus

---

50   Stephen Pattemore, "God So Loved the Cosmos," in *Creation and Hope*, ed. Nicola Hoggard-Creegan and Andrew Shepherd (Eugene, OR, Pickwick Publications, 2018), p. 121.

25). A thought-provoking verse is, "The lions roar for their prey and seek their food from God" (Psalm 104:21).

The Psalmist adds "How many are your works, O Lord; in wisdom you made them all" Psalm 124:4). What God made he loves, and what he loves he will redeem—the whole world.

Jesus constantly related earth to heaven, as seen in the Lord's Prayer. ("Your will be done on earth as it is in heaven.") All too often we have kept God the Creator at a distance. We may accept his laws such as gravity and the gift of life itself, but we treat him as a distant God who created the universe and left it to run according to his timeless laws. This is seen in the concept of gravity by Francis Bacon (1561-1656).

Secular people keep God out of their lives and suppress their moral conscience. In many cases they call on God only as death approaches.

As we have seen, Lynn White accused Christians of exploiting nature and misinterpreting the phrase "to have dominion over it" (Genesis 1). He said Christians believed nature's only purpose was to serve mankind.

While it is sometimes true that Christians have dominated nature for selfish reasons, White's accusation misunderstands the intent of the two concepts of dominion, that is, to rule and to subdue the earth (Genesis 1, 26-28). Both are needed in a sin-infested world, one positive (to rule) and the other negative (to subdue).

The Rights of Animals, Birds and Fish

Animals, birds and fish have the breath of life, as do human beings. We have a limited understanding of how animals suffer. We do know that herds of jungle animals such as elephants go to the same location to die, as do birds.

A much-loved Psalm (23) speaks of the love of a shepherd, as expanded in John 10. Jesus loved the world of nature. He speaks of the birds that neither sow nor reap, and the lilies that clothe the fields but do not spin (Matthew 6:25-32.) God knows the value of the humble sparrow. (Matthew 10:29-30). Much of Jesus' brief ministry was given to restoring the goodness of creation. He healed the sick and diseased, fed the hungry, liberated young and old from demonic oppression, raised the dead to life, and exercised his control over nature when he calmed the Sea of Galilee in order to save the lives of his disciples.

Animals, birds and fish, as sentient beings, have the right to care and protection by people over whom the Creator has given the moral right of stewardship. For example, the farmer must not muzzle the ox while it is treading out the corn (Deuteronomy 25:40.) When God told Adam to name all the livestock, the birds of the air and the beasts of the field (Genesis 2:19-20), he was suggesting human beings had the authority to rule over nature.

It seems that at the beginning, humans were vegetarian, but with the introduction of the sacrificial system, salvation was symbolized by the killing of spotless animals whose meat was eaten by priests and worshippers. The Deuteronomic laws distinguished between clean and unclean animals for eating. This principle is continued today by Jews and Muslims. Some experts believe that the Covid-19 disease began in China with the eating of unclean meat such as bats, purchased in the marketplace.

Christians have a moral responsibility to honour the rights of all God's sentient creatures, recognising that human beings are a separate category, being made in God's image. In our modern world these creation rights are being greatly abused. For example, wild elephants are being mercilessly killed by poachers for their tusks, and rhinos for their horns, Domesticated animals and birds need human care. This is sometimes ignored in zoos and circuses. It is immoral to keep hens in battery conditions for their meat and eggs. Christians should campaign for free-range eggs and free-range chicken meat. Birds should not be kept in small cages for their owners' pleasure, nor fish in very restricted aquariums.

At the same time the sanctity of human life must be protected. When we Christians do little to restrain death through abortion, suicide and euthanasia, we are failing in our moral responsibilities. Moreover, those who practise idolatry by worshipping the elements of creation and not the Creator will be judged.

The good news is that God will redeem and restore his creation at the return of Jesus Christ to reign on the earth. Isaiah prophesied that the wolf would live with the lamb and the leopard would lie down with the goat (11:6). This is repeated in Isaiah 65:24-25. This promise will be fulfilled at the coming of the new heaven and the new earth.

The Awe of Creation

Psalm 8 begins and ends with:

> "O Lord Our God, how majestic is your name in all the earth!"

In awe the Psalmist looks at the heavens, the moon and the stars and marvels that God has created human beings a little lower than the heavenly beings and that he has given humankind dominion over all creation.

Robert Meye adds:

"To contemplate nature is an invitation to wonder."[51] He outlines the parameters of a theology of nature, beginning with contemplating the wonder of the triune God as Father, Son and Holy Spirit.

While animals and humans have a common DNA at differing levels, people are unique because God created them in his own image, male and female (Genesis 1:26-27). God blessed them and commanded them to increase in numbers, to rule over all other life and subdue what is evil. The forceful nature of these two terms, to "rule" and to "subdue," in the Hebrew, points to the essential nature of our human stewardship. Although these two terms have been both abused and misunderstood, both are important for human beings to fulfil the purposes for which God created them.

God is a triune community of persons who give purpose and meaning to life. In his unity of being, God created the unity of creation. When I walk through Auckland's forested Waitakere Ranges, I marvel at the harmony of the life of the trees and plants, each growing towards the light above. They each reproduce exactly according to their kind. Their common life and unity of purpose reflects the glory of God. I am also in awe of the amazing abilities of human beings created in the image of God to talk to their creator and to discuss with one another deep philosophical concepts. At the same time, I enjoy the beauty of nature, its colours, shapes and smells.

The problem is, we are in danger of turning our God-given dominion into unjust domination and misusing creation for our own selfish ends. No wonder it is "groaning and longing for liberation" (Romans 8:18-27). God grieves when we abuse his world. We marvel at his ability to remake us as new creatures in his image. We are the recipients of his grace, not the creators of it.

The progression from Day One to Day Six of creation is a divine miracle of the continuity of creation. Science may explain how this happens, but only God can tell us why and for what purpose. The uniqueness of God's creation is that "humankind needs nature more than nature needs humankind."[52]

Human beings were created for thought, art and work, among other giftings. Religious art uniquely reflects the distinctions of each culture. Human creativity is at the heart of modern science and philosophy. As humans we love beauty in the shape, colour and smell of flowers, the perfect

---

[51]   Robert Meye, "Invitation to Wonder: Towards a Theology of Nature" In *Tending the Garden*, ed. Wesley Granberg- Michaelson (Grand Rapids, MI: Eerdmans, 1990), p. 31.

[52]   Ibid., p. 47.

crystals of the snow, the sound of the waterfall and the harmony of the colours of the rainbow. God has blessed us beyond our expectation and has given us the earth as our home. No other planet in our solar system has life as we on earth have it.

The Gift of Language and Reason

God has blessed us with the gift of language, with its complicated grammars and limitless words with a variety of meanings. While birds and animals communicate with each other in ways we don't understand, human language is unique. We assume when we pray in our own language that God hears and answers our prayers.

Again, human beings have the capacity to reason logically, to reflect on the past and to envisage the future. This is unique to our kind. For many people the ability to reason defines their identity, while for others their emotions define theirs.

Conscience

Conscience is a guide and judge of moral action. It is our inner sense of what we understand to be right and wrong. It is an important aspect of being created in the image of God, and it is inherent in all people. Moreover. it is a universal moral indicator for justice in society. It recognizes general rules for peaceful communal living and is the ground for deciding particular cases of behaviour. Conscience usually motivates people for better marriage and family life and discipline in sexual relationships. In this way it is both a guide for how we should live and a judge of wrong motives and actions. Moreover, the compassionate treatment of animals and the preservation of the fertility of the land are areas where the rule of conscience is needed.

On several occasions Jesus appealed to the conscience of the Pharisees, although he didn't use the term "conscience." Paul went on to comment that when the Gentiles (non-Jews) who didn't have the written law of Moses, understood what the law required. They were responding to the law written on their hearts, which either accused or defended them (Romans 2:14-16),

Conscience is not perfect, however. It can be misunderstood or ignored because of the sinful nature of the human heart. People can be oversensitive, afraid of making moral decisions for fear of offending others, or they may have a weak conscience to excuse their own evil actions. This latter is the danger, for example, of extreme religious and political organisations found in every religion. By contrast, Christians need to appeal to the Holy Spirit to renew and guide their consciences in matters of right and wrong. Paul warns against becoming a stumbling block to those who have a weak conscience over eating meat that has been sacrificed to idols (Romans 8:1-13).

Thus, we marvel that earth is our common home. We share its resources and we depend on it for our life. Book 5 of the Psalms (chapters 146-150) ends with a shout of praise and thanksgiving to God:

"Let everything that has breath praise the Lord." (Psalm 150:6)

This includes the whole of creation.

Our Shared Relationships

Understanding God as the Creator of all living beings is the entry point to our understanding of this world as our shared home. The world can be pictured as a triangle of shared relationships whose pinnacle is God and whose base is human beings and nature. To be truly human we have to relate to both God and nature. A human being existing in isolation on a desert island is not fully human.

Scripture records a Pharisee coming to Jesus to test him on the greatest commandment. Jesus' response was not to challenge the Mosaic law. He went first to Deuteronomy 6:4 which calls for loving God with all our heart and soul and strength. Then he turned to Leviticus 19:18 which reads: "Love your neighbour as yourself." Jesus then added that all the Law and Prophets hung on these two commandments (Matthew 22:33-40). Regarding this instruction to love both God and one's neighbour, Jesus told the lawyer to go and do likewise (Luke 10:37).

The Pharisees were experts in the Law and strong on ethics but weak in relating both to life.[53] Jesus' point was that if we don't love our neighbour, we don't really love God. When asked, "Who is my neighbour?" Jesus said it was the person in physical need, and then he told the story of the Good Samaritan (Luke 10:30-37). Compassionate action is the evidence of genuine love.

God's requirement for faithfulness became evident in the covenant he initiated with Abraham, who responded in love and obedience. For his part, God promised Abraham the land of Canaan as an everlasting

---

[53]   Michael Green, *The Message of Matthew* (Leicester, Inter-Varsity, 2000), p. 36.

possession for him and his descendants, but on the condition that they kept their part of the covenant (Genesis 17:1-8). The relationship between God and Abraham was implied in the words, "I will be your God and you shall be my people."

This was the covenant that transformed this minor community into an international force. It continues to the present day, where Israel defines its identity in its hereditary right to the land of Israel and keeps the Sabbath Day as a day of rest for both the people and their animals.

The Transformation of Global Suffering

Suffering and pain are common to all life on the planet, animal and human. Suffering creates fear. Animals fear each other, and birds constantly look in all directions as they search for food. Most people are tribal, with a history of killing one another. Greed and racial pride lead to wars between communities, increasing pain and suffering. Unless pain is cured it leads to death.

Buddha, who had no belief in God, recognised a fundamental principle that all life is *dukkha* or suffering. In his first sermon at Benares he reportedly said, "Now this, O monks, is the first noble truth: birth is painful, old age and death are painful, contact with unpleasant things is painful, not getting what one wishes for is painful." Although Buddha recognised the value of happiness, joy and lovingkindness, he said that when these passed away life returned to pain and suffering.

These insights into the negative side of life have been shared throughout human history, from the early Greek philosophers, to the Enlightenment, to contemporary life. In some cases, pain is incurable and death seems to be the only answer. Moreover, many campaigners for euthanasia believe death is the end of all pain and existence and that there is no life beyond it.

Buddha understood that the cause of suffering was complex. In his Second Noble Truth he analysed its causes as *tanha*, or desire, thirst and craving. He concluded that craving was for sensual pleasures, success in life, and the annihilation of the self (non-existence). The goal was to achieve *nirvana*, the extinction of life itself, by following the Fourth Noble Truth, the Eightfold Path. This included the avoidance of extremes and the suppression of all desires through discipline and ongoing meditation. The way to overcome attachment to desire was to recognise that "every moment you are born, you decay and you die."

Christians may agree with some of Buddha's insights on the nature of suffering, but we sharply differ on how to overcome it. Buddha's answer was to extinguish suffering, as one puts out a flame on a candle. Hindus turn to their many gods to achieve *bhakti* as deliverance from the self and from pain and rebirth. Animists seek freedom from suffering by placating evil spirits.

For the Christian, suffering takes on a different meaning, for it leads to new life and meaningful death. We first understand what happened to Adam and Eve. When they ate the forbidden fruit, they sinned against God and began to suffer. The snake became human beings' first enemy. Women lost their equality with men and desired to be ruled by them; thorns and thistles grew out of control, and the farmer through "painful toil" had to cultivate the land before he could enjoy its fruit (Genesis 3:17-19).

Adam and Eve died spiritually the day they sinned, but Adam lived on physically for another 930 years. For the Christian, the sting of death is overcome when God gives us the victory of new life through our Lord Jesus Christ. We know that nothing can separate us from the love of God.

Christ was the Suffering Servant of Isaiah 53, a man of sorrows and familiar with suffering. When Christ suffered, God suffered. When God raised Christ on the third day, he became the model to believers of their own resurrection to abundant new life. Then God gave him a name above every name, that before him every knee should bow (Philippians 2:10).

Paul states, "The sting of death is sin. But thanks be to God who gives us the victory through our Lord Jesus Christ. Therefore, stand firm. Let nothing move you." (1 Corinthians 15:56-58).

Jesus said, "Blessed are those who are persecuted because of righteousness, for theirs is the kingdom of heaven" (Matthew 5:8). Suffering will be transformed into peace and joy.

The biblical story of honour and shame, sin and guilt

From Genesis to Revelation the two concepts of honour/shame and sin/guilt are integrated. God put Adam and Eve in the garden to work in it and enjoy its fruit, except for two trees, one symbolizing the knowledge of good and evil and the other the possession of eternal life. They were naked and unashamed. But after they had disobeyed God's law and sinned, their eyes were opened to their nakedness and they were ashamed. They had nowhere to hide, and they sought to cover their nakedness with fig leaves. Their shame led to guilt. They tried to hide from God when God said to them, "Where are you?" (Genesis 3:9). They first blamed each other and then the serpent. God expelled them from the Garden, increased the woman's pain in childbirth, while Adam had to battle the thorns and thistles by the sweat of his brow.

The continuing stories in Genesis 4 to 11 indicate the continuing relationship between the two concepts.

An example of this relationship was when the prophet Nathan rebuked King David for his adultery with Bathsheba. At the same time, he shamed him with the story of the rich man who took the poor man's only ewe lamb to feed a guest. In telling words, Nathan said to the king, "You are the man" (2 Samuel 12:7). The king confessed his shame and guilt to Nathan, saying, "I have sinned against the Lord."

The same interrelatedness runs through the New Testament. Jesus in the Sermon on the Mount and in his parables and in the healing of all who suffered, appealed to both shame and guilt. The parable of the prodigal son illustrates his shame and longing for forgiveness, whereas the elder son, who had not been given the same family privileges as his younger brother, felt dishonoured and humiliated.

On the cross, the symbol of Roman shame, Jesus was humiliated by being crucified naked, but the act of his dying and being raised to life on the third day restored the honour of God. In conservative Christianity, Jesus' death is portrayed only as an atonement for sin, with little if any reference to honour and shame. But the writer to the Hebrews urges that we fix our eyes on Jesus, the author and finisher of our faith, "who for the joy set before him endured the cross, *despising its shame*, and sat down at the right hand of the throne of God" (Hebrews 12:2).

In India, Ken Gnanakan is one who recognises the need for balance between law and guilt and honour and shame in the context of understanding the importance of sustaining and restoring God's creation. The same emphasis was made by Nehemiah Goreh and K.M. Banerjea in the nineteenth century, and today in India by Ivan Satyavrata and by Vishal Mangalwadi. In today's society we also need a theology that embrace the cosmos of God the creator, sustainer, judge and redeemer of all of life.

Chapter 5: Asian Religious Response to Creation Care

Every human being is created in the image and likeness of God (Genesis 1:26). So all people are equal in God's sight, regardless of ethnicity, religion and economic status. We are called to respect and honour each other's and our own society, of which the basis is the human family.

The challenge of this chapter is to understand the diversity and common values of world religions. This is a search for common values and a common global ethic in religious movements, to reduce the gap between rich and poor and to help the increasing number of people suffering from oppressive economic, political and social forces.

Religions are becoming more divisive, however, as seen in the rise of fundamentalist Islam with its aggressive jihadist believers, while in the present political stance of the BJP ruling party in India an Indian must be a Hindu to be an Indian. In Myanmar and Si Lanka, Buddhist fundamentalists are openly attacking both Christians and Muslims.

The Deification of Nature

The most common human response to nature is to deify it. Nature becomes a cosmic, impersonal reality which has neither beginning nor end. It is eternal. In religious terms, nature as Mother Earth becomes the goddess with whom worshippers can identify. Nature becomes an idol that the worshippers use for their own religious ends. All appearances are maya (unreal).

Sadly, modern science has no place for the supernatural. Newton and Descartes believed in the deistic autonomy of the laws of nature. They had little recognition of God's continual intervention in creation. For them, miracles didn't happen.

Einstein believed in the interchangeability of matter and energy. His quantum physics has been used by Fritjof Capra and Gary Zukav to support a monistic view of nature. *The Tao of Physics* by Capra and *The Dancing Wu Li Masters* by Zukav support the view that the mind determines all things. Their god is timeless energy. Nataraja, the dancing Shiva of Hinduism, symbolizes this timeless reality.

This philosophic view of reality became religious pantheism in which god is all and all is god. Nature is spiritualized, as seen in the worship of

Mother Earth in New Age religions. Religious knowledge is achieved by identifying with and experiencing cosmic reality.

Gaia (the name for the Greek goddess of the earth) is a scientific thesis developed by Jim Lovelock, a NASA scientist in the 1960s. He tried to show how nature was a self-organizing and self-regulating entity and a self-perpetuating organism. An example of this principle is the delicate balance maintained between the levels of oxygen and carbon needed to maintain life. The tropical rainforests are the lungs of the earth. They absorb carbon dioxide and give off the oxygen that is needed for all animal life. These gases exist in an equilibrium state. Gaia as a goddess has been adopted by New Age pantheists as evidence that god is everything and everything is god. For others, religion itself is pantheistic, for everything is in god and god is in everything.

This view of Gaia as sacred earth was heavily canvassed at the Earth Summit at Rio de Janeiro in 1992, where Mother Earth religion was promoted as the ethic to save the earth from human destruction.

Our calling as Christians, by contrast, is to rule over creation in ways that are accountable to God and to subdue the evils in the world for which we are responsible. Christ calls us to repent and believe the gospel, not to deify Mother Earth. The earth ethic cannot reverse the ill effects of climate change because it does not counter the sinful forces dominating our world. For some people evil does not exist, or it is defined as a lack of knowledge. But the impact of evil on human society is seen in the degree of hate and violence to which human beings descend. A positive ethic built on faith in a just and loving creator God is needed if evil is to be restrained and good implemented both in society and on the land.

The Secular Viewpoint

Today, secularism, like a pandemic virus, is spreading throughout the world. It ignores the presence of God in people's daily lives. It reminds me of a hoarding I saw on a railway bridge in Auckland which said:

> There is probably no God.
> Don't let religion divide us.
> Let us enjoy life together.

Secularism urges us to exclude religion from civil affairs and all public education so that religion becomes only a private activity. Eventually secularism becomes hostile to all religious activity, especially Christian activity. Historically, secularism was active in the Golden Age of Greek philosophy led by Socrates, Plato and Aristotle. They made the self with its senses the rational goal of living. Secularism also became a motif of the Enlightenment, when God was acknowledged as a distant creator who could only be known through the laws of nature and by reason.

Secularism has devastated the church in the western world, reducing church attendance to a fraction of what it was seventy-five years ago. It has relegated Christianity to the fringes of the modern world. Sadly, the church is powerless to confront the global issues of violence, sexual abuse and corruption in commercial and industrial life.

The most coherent and aggressive form of atheism and anti-Christian spirituality has been preached at every opportunity by Richard Dawkins of Oxford University, as indicated in his book, *The God Delusion*. In 2015 Dawkins argued that children needed protection from the religious views of their parents, but by 2018 he was having second thoughts. He was alarmed by the rising violence in society, the irrational behaviour of youth and the destruction of the environment, and began to fear a global meltdown. Dawkins came to admit, "People may feel free to do bad things because they fear God is no longer watching them."[54]

Mao Zedong, architect of the communist revolution in China (1950-1976), once said, "Man's ability to know and change Nature is unlimited." Mao was the saviour-god. His *Little Red Book* was the bible which everybody had to read and recite. Social justice was his ethic. His economic utopia was heaven, to be achieved by self-sacrifice and submission to the state. During the Mao years, there was extreme human interference in the natural world, and Taoist religions were severely repressed. Under Mao, the traditional Chinese ideal of "harmony between heaven and humans" was abrogated in favour of Mao's insistence that "man must conquer nature." Mao and the Chinese Communist Party's "war" to bend the physical world to human will had disastrous consequences both for human beings and for the natural environment. China is responsible for one of the world's worst environmental disasters. It is the world's largest emitter of carbon dioxide, and some of the cities have so much smog that people need to wear masks outside.[55]

There is today a growing disillusionment with secularism and with human-centred spirituality. The utopian project of creating a society based on faith in ourselves is failing. The secularist needs to return to a Christian worldview and a religious ethic is becoming increasingly necessary. One

54   From an article in *The Times*, October 5, 2019.
55   Shapiro, Judith, *Mao's War Against Nature: Politics and the Environment in Revolutionary China*. Cambridge University Press, 2001, p. 68.

fact that is intensifying the need for God is the steady decline of peace and harmony in the ecological world. The reality is that the politicians and the scientists are having only a limited influence in changing the global climatic situation. Extreme weather patterns are increasing, pandemics multiplying, people are suffering increasingly from disease, and many are starving to death. Many in the world are beginning to realize they need a transcendent God.

Secular people demand freedom of choice to make life-changing decisions. But while riches and pleasure may be sought after, they do not guarantee inner peace. Instead, Jesus says, "Come to me and I will give you rest." He alone fulfils the longing of the human heart. In him the sacred/secular divide no longer exists, for he is Lord of both heaven and earth.

The Religious Search to Restore the Earth

Multicultural Religions

As we have seen, Maurice Strong, director of the Earth Summit, appealed to religions to help solve the environmental crisis. He wanted to see moral, ethical and spiritual values at the centre of individual and societal lives.

We turn now to consider how far the main religions of Asia and their leadership have achieved peace and justice for their people and for their lands.

Tribal Spirit worship

From pre-history the tribal peoples of the world have been spirit worshippers. Spirits occupy the whole of nature; there are no empty spaces. Tribals have an inherent awareness of good and evil spirits, and they spend their lives meeting the needs of the good ones and placating the evil ones. These people are generally *henotheist*, seeking to please one god among the many they worship. In order to cover their own failings and evil behaviour, they sacrifice animals instead of killing other people.

Harold Turner writes: "Many tribal people are much more religious than many westerners. They live close to nature and sense its mysterious powers."[56]

---

[56]   Harold Turner, "World of the Spirits." In *The World's Religions* (Grand Rapids, Eerdmans, 1982), p. 128.

In their awareness of real human need, tribals have "the hallmarks of true religion."[57] Terms such as animism and paganism do not adequately define their true religious nature. Their ancestors are known as the "living dead" who must be worshipped and whose material needs must be met. Priests or "medicine men" have supernatural powers to ward off evil spirits and to interpret the blessings of the good ones. The Aboriginals of Australia are a living example of a tribal people who have a profound respect for the forces of the natural world. From a biblical perspective, tribal people in their worship repeat both the creative and degenerate stories recorded in Genesis 1-11.

Demonic Power

Demonic power differs from pagan spirit worship. Demons are evil powers used by witches, sorcerers, magicians, and fortune tellers to change the direction of people's lives. They are active in all Asian and African religious traditions and in other religious traditions as well.

Hindus, Buddhists and adherents of folk Islam are constantly striving against the world of demons. One of the most loved Hindu myths is the story of Rama, the king of Ayodhya. He is the hero of the Ramayana. While he and his beautiful and chaste wife Sita were in the forest, the demon Ravana kidnapped Sita and took her to Sri Lanka. In an attempt to rescue her, Rama killed Ravana. This story plays an important part in the lives of village people. Demons have to be kept out of the village, for they are responsible for disease and epidemics.

Buddha was plagued from the night of his Enlightenment by Mara, an evil spirit, who tempted him not to tell others about his Enlightenment. During his following six weeks of meditation, Buddha was constantly troubled by this spirit. In Buddhist art the most popular painting is of Mara, the demon of passion and death. Thus, the spirit world is very real to many religions. It is even more real to pagans who spend their lives seeking to placate the spirits.

Hinduism

The rishi philosophers who shaped the Vedas of 3500 to 4000 years ago, were deeply religious and spiritual in their search for ultimate truth. As authors of the Vedas, they viewed the Scriptures as *sruti*, as the *sanatana dharma* or eternal word of God. As both philosophers and religionists, they

---

[57]   Ibid., p. 129.

wrote what they "heard" in silence and saw truth as it was. They strove to worship the One Supreme God whom they saw being represented in several elements of nature, especially Agni the god of fire, Indira, the storm god, and Varuna the chief god who controlled the cosmic order. In each case they were gods of nature, with whom the rishis identified and to whom they looked for maintaining peace and order on the earth. At the same time, the rishis emphasized sacrifice to restore the cosmic order and for the forgiveness of sins. Hinduism has little knowledge of demons. The closest to an evil spirit was the non-Aryan *Rudra*, the storm god of the Rigveda.

The movement from the Vedic religion to philosophy was slow and barely perceptible. The change culminated in the Upanishads, at the end of the Vedic period. Much later, the two great interpreters, Shankara (788-820 AD) and Ramanuja (1077-1137 AD), with their doctrine of nondual Vedanta, reflected their philosophical understanding of the One Ultimate Reality. Brahman, the impersonal and eternal One, was in unity with Atman, the Self or eternal soul. By contrast, the empirical self, or the body, was less than real. It was *maya* or an illusion of the mind. Shankara defined this Oneness as *nirguna*, without attributes, while Ramanuja described Oneness as *saguna*, with attributes. The latter included the gods and goddesses and nature itself. To treat nature as real was *avidya* or ignorance. Clearly, this philosophical approach resulted in indifference to the ecological crisis of their time. They had no desire to redeem nature from its corruption.

Saguna-centred religion led to *ahimsa*, nonviolence towards all of life, human and subhuman. The Jain Hindu sect took ahimsa literally, seeking to avoid the death of the smallest insect. Ahimsa became the motivating principle of Mahatma Gandhi who emphasized it in his call to maintain harmony and identity with nature.

Hindus are now being challenged to widen their traditional concept of *dharma* (the right way of living) and *samsara*, (continual rebirth), to include responsibility for family and caste, for peace and justice in society, and increasingly for the care of nature. They recognize that human suffering is not only the consequence of behaviour in a previous life but also of the abuse of the environment in which they now live.

Swami Vivekanandavol (1862-1902) represented Hinduism at the first World Parliament of Religions, held in Chicago in 1893. In the opening session, Vivekananda began his address with the words, "Sisters and brothers of America" for which he received a two-minute ovation. In the name of Hinduism, which he called "the mother of religion" he appealed for tolerance and universal acceptance of all religions. However, he made no reference to any abuse of the land.

That did not come until 100 years later, at the Second Parliament of Religions in Chicago in 1993. Since then, a World Parliament of Religion has been held every five years, first in Cape Town (1999), and then Barcelona (2004), Melbourne (2009) and Salt Lake City (2015.) After that they were to be held every two years. Although eight to ten thousand people attend each parliament, its global influence seems limited. Issues have centred on women's freedom, traditional marriage and justice, but they have shown little concern for creation care. Even the United Nations founding charter in 1945, with its Universal Declaration of Human Rights in 1948, had no reference to ecological issues.

While Hinduism continues to advocate the harmony of religions, its concern for environmental issues, including climate change, is only a recent development, perhaps largely the result of Christian and secular calls for action. India has done little to implement the decisions of the Paris Accord. New Delhi was one of the most beautiful cities in Asia, with a high standard of living and free-flowing traffic. Now it is the most polluted city in the world, even worse than Beijing.

However, there have been individual reformers whose campaigns for equality and social justice have spilled over into environmental issues. In India we mention the names of Ram Mohan Roy and the Brahma Samaj who were attracted to the Christian ethic and the care of the environment, Sri Aurobindo with his ashram at Pondicherry, and the devotional poet, Rabindranath Tagore, who developed an ashram at Shantiniketan, Bengal. And, of course, there was Mahatma Gandhi and Dr Radhakrishnan of Madras (now Chennai.) Each of them developed ashrams where their members could peacefully relate to nature. In present day India two contemporary evangelical Christian scholars may be mentioned for their outstanding commitment to creation care: Vishal Mangalwadi and Ken Gnanakan.

Buddhism

Buddhism is a secular way of life, offering spirituality without reference to God. The Buddhist involvement with environmental issues began with the Buddha himself. He was a fervent evangelist for identification and harmony with nature. He was compassionate about human suffering, for in the First Noble Truth he described all life as suffering. However, the care of nature was limited to the work of the monks who cared for the gardens attached to their monasteries. Buddha's concern for liberation from suffering was to be achieved by following the Eightfold Path. He showed little concern for the renewal of nature itself.

In east Asia, the followers of Taoism, Confucianism and the pure Land and Zen Buddhist sects, as with Shintoism, all emphasized the seeking of the unity and harmony between their religion and nature. The Japanese water gardens and their tea ceremonies, are models of this search for harmony.

Nevertheless, neither Hinduism nor Buddhism have made any significant contribution to reducing our global crisis. Under political and global pressure, they identified with the Paris Accord to reduce the levels of carbon and limit the increase in global temperatures, but in practice there is little evidence of change in their policies and activities.

Oriental Vitalism

Common to all oriental religious beliefs and practices is the reality of a universal "life force" which can act for the good of humanity or destroy life. It flows through the universe with intelligence and power and is an alternative to monotheistic interpretations of the supernatural and of miracles.[58] In Chinese religion the life force is known as *Qi*, or *Ch'i*; in Hinduism it is *prana*; in Korea it is part of *shamanism*. In each of these traditions there is no creator god, only nature's invisible life force which flows through the universe. It is nonphysical and cannot be investigated by science, though in science fiction it is the "Force" as in the Star Wars films. Disease is the result of disturbing the flow of energy in the body. It can be manipulated and healed. In Chinese religion this is by meditation, massage, and acupuncture. In Indian religion it is through ayurvedic medicine.

Daoism, also called Taoism, is the indigenous philosophical and religious system of China. Tao, translated as "The Way," was shaped by Lao-Tzu in the sixth century BC and by I Ching in Classic of Changes, as an ancient manual of divination.[59] This concept of the life force must be kept in a balance between the *yin*, the female passive power of the universe, and the *yang*, the male active power of the cosmos.

Maintaining this balance is at the heart of the Chinese Taoist concern for the environment. It shaped their response to the present climate crisis. Chinese religion focuses on maintaining a harmony with the natural forces, not transforming them.

---

[58]   P C Reisser, "New Age Therapies" from *The Dictionary of Contemporary Religion in the Western World* (Leicester, Inter Varsity Press, 2002), pp. 283-285.

[59]   Ibid. C.W. Weber, "Daoism", pp. 223-226.

Taoism is eclectic. It has profoundly influenced the other two Chinese religions, Confucianism and Buddhism. Chinese religion today is the integration of all three.

Confucianism is a social and practical interpretation of "The Way," based on the five hierarchical family relationships. Filial piety is the most important virtue, and basic to social morality.

The Post-Modernity of the New Age

At the end of the 19th century the philosopher Nietzsche pronounced "God is dead and we have killed him."[60]

The harmonizing of western and Asian subjectivism has led to the development of New Age spirituality filling the religious void in the minds and hearts of many western secularists and those dissatisfied with their traditional religious faith.

The key to understanding the New Age movement begins with understanding *karma*, the spiritual principle of cause and effect. To understand karma is to take responsibility for our spiritual self.[61] Health and wealth are for those who are spiritually enlightened. *Samsara*, as reincarnation, also means that New Agers can choose their future spiritual state.

This interpretation of spirituality is applied to the people of the New Age and their identity with nature. Because the physical world is *maya* or unreal, these people believe they can influence it by the power of the mind. They have little interest in renewing or liberating nature but try to control climate change with their minds. New Agers see themselves as belonging to the Age of Aquarius in which expanding self-consciousness has replaced the so-called Christian age of Pisces. Their monistic thinking has nothing constructive to say about our ecological crisis.

Nevertheless, since all of humanity has been made in the image of God the Creator, all people are in fact religious whether they acknowledge it or not. Our ongoing task is to recognize the diversity of religious beliefs and practices and the search for common values and to respond with a Christian perspective of the personal, creator, sustainer, redeemer God.

---

[60] Steve Hollinghurst, *New Age Paganism and Christian Mission* (Cambridge, Grove Books, 2003) 6. This booklet is EV 64 in the Evangelism series of Grove Books and is a concise but practical insight into the current ideology of post-modernity. It is especially helpful in analysing the New Age and the Christian response to it.

[61] Ibid., p. 11.

Monotheistic Religions

The real challenge to respond to the suffering planet comes from the three monotheistic religions of Judaism, Christianity and Islam. Each has a common belief in the transcendent God who is personal, eternal and the creator of all that exists. This belief in God as the creator is the key to their engagement with the needs of creation. For the monotheists the universe had a beginning and is moving towards an end, a reality that some scientists also acknowledge. This belief in God as the creator is the bedrock of the monotheistic religions' care for creation. The world is not only *creatio ex nihilo* (made out of nothing); it is also being sustained by God the creator. The followers of these faiths recognize that God will hold them accountable for their stewardship or care of creation.

These three religions, whose origin is in Asia or the Middle East, look to their scriptures for guidance—the Old Testament for Jews, the whole Bible for Christians, and the Qur'an for Muslims. Each religion seeks to fulfil its responsibility to care for and rule over nature and to subdue the evils which are destroying it. While they don't agree on each other's path to reconciliation with their creator God, they do agree on their common responsibility to act justly for the liberation of Planet Earth from its groanings. They each have a desire to harmonize their faith with their lifestyle and action. Faith motivates good action and each is a living faith. James in his letter stresses the interdependence of faith and life, which cannot be separated although they are distinct (James 2:24). Asians look for a harmony of relationships with people and with nature rather than a confrontation with them.

Judaism

Judaism began with Abraham being called out of the pagan city of Ur of the Chaldees to enjoy a special relationship with God the creator, based on his holy and just laws. God told Abraham to leave his country and his relatives and go to a land that he would show him. There in Palestine (Canaan) God made a covenant with him, and promised him the land for his descendants. From then on this became a symbol of the Hebrews' identity in the land now called Israel. Politically they will never agree to a division of their land into two nations.

Then God's promise came to Solomon on the night of the dedication of the temple, when God said, "If my people who are called by my name will humble themselves and pray and seek my face and turn from their wicked ways, then I will hear from heaven and forgive their sins and heal their land (2 Chronicle 7:14). The healing of the land became the nation's aspiration.

The keeping of the weekly Sabbath day of rest was the Hebrews' commitment to God, to acknowledge that he was the owner of the land and they were his tenants. The principle of the Sabbath renewal of the land culminated with the promise of a Jubilee Year when the land would be rested, and harmony re-established between landowners and their land. (Leviticus 25:8-55. Israel's recovery of their desert lands is now a model for other nations. They have made the desert bloom and are now exporting their fruit.

The prophet Isaiah promised that God would eventually redeem his creation to the point where the wolf and the lamb would feed together and the lion would eat straw like the ox (Isaiah 65:24-25). This is a foretaste of a new heaven and a new earth, promised to Isaiah and repeated in Revelation 21 and 22. It is yet to be fulfilled, waiting for the return of Jesus Christ to earth.

Islam

Christians would do well to learn from some aspects of Islamic spirituality, especially trust in God and worship centring on prayer. The success of Islam is due to its confident trust in Almighty God and its strict obedience to divine sharia law. Muslims are confident that the summa (the community of Muslims) will eventually control the whole world.

Islam's engagement in the ecological crisis is a recent development, no doubt under pressure from Christian engagement and perhaps even more from the global secular community with its environmental conferences and laws.

In preparation for the Paris consultation of November to December 2015, Islamic leaders sponsored an International Islamic Climate Change symposium in Istanbul, Turkey. In August 2015, three months before the Paris meeting, Muslim nations promised to phase out the use of all fossil fuels and shift to 100 percent renewable sources of energy. They then endorsed the Paris Agreement. But along with all other communities, they have shown little action to control the level of carbon.

In Malaysia and Indonesia, the Muslim rulers have approved the cutting down of the primal forests to replace them with palm trees for their rich oil. Palm trees are low in oxygen production compared to primal forests. The globalization of Islam through migration and the flood of refugees to Europe has brought Muslims into direct conflict with the nations that are striving to reduce their greenhouse gases. Saudi Arabia and other

Islamic oil-producing nations plan to increase their production of oil, not reduce it.

The Sunni and Shi'a nations are now in conflict with each other in Iraq and Yemen. In the destruction of the land, they are releasing vast quantities of carbon into the air. At the same time the Islamic nations are doing little to restrain the radical Jihadist elements which are causing enormous physical and environmental destruction in many countries. Their involvement in the Israel/Palestine conflict distracts them from any effort to care for the environment in Palestine and the neighbouring countries. It is evident that Islam's prior concern is to continue to spread its faith globally, to have worldwide acceptance of its sharia-law and to see the expansion of their umma into one global religious community.

The hope is that Christians can work with moderate Muslims so that together they can liberate nature from its groaning and bring peace and harmony to their lands. A common program to restore the forests, lower the level of carbon in the air and to support each other's policy to reduce the level of fossil fuels in global use is to be encouraged. They need to work together in responding to cyclones, floods, droughts and fire.

Christianity

Of all the world religions, Christianity has the strongest message about our obligation to care for creation and to work for the liberation of planet Earth from its "groanings." Christian hope for planet Earth is built on three principles:

First, God is the creator and sustainer of the earth and all life on it. The cosmos had a beginning and it will climax with the return of Jesus Christ to the earth as judge and king.

Secondly, God is a just and living covenant-keeping God. He will redeem his creation by judging evil and rewarding righteousness on the earth. At the cross Jesus inaugurated a new covenant of love and compassion. In the resurrection we glimpse the wonder of the new creation and are amazed that Jesus took the marks of his humanity with him to heaven. The new covenant widens our concept of the land from that controlled by Israel to include the whole world, where in God's timing the kingdoms of the world would become "the kingdom of our Lord and of his Christ" (Revelation 11:15)

Thirdly the biblical hope for Planet Earth is that God plans to liberate it from its human abuse, purify it, and establish a new earth, based on righteousness. This will begin with the return of Jesus Christ. Christianity offers hope beyond the present climatic crisis. Scientists who would like to control the level of carbon dioxide have little evidence to show that this is happening, at least in the developed world. Christians believe that God alone can save the planet from imploding in self-destruction.

God and nature are not one reality, materially or spiritually. In no sense did God ever become impersonal nature or did nature become God. The earth and all the universe had a beginning in time and space because God alone is eternal, the transcendent creator of all that exists.

The amazing reality is that in the Incarnation God chose to become one with his creation, not by merging with it but by sending Jesus Christ as his Son who is truly God and truly human. God came not as an imaginary "mother" to be worshipped as an idol of our sinful hearts. Jesus' unique accomplishment as the God-man was to destroy the evil in the world and to redeem human beings who were made in his image but who were now enslaved in self-centred idolatry.

Chapter 6: The Institutional Care of Creation

June 23, 1988, marked the date when climate change became a global issue. On that day, Dr James Hansen, the director of NASA's Institute for Space Studies, testified to the US Congress that global warming was caused by human pollution and the exploitation of carbon resources, resulting in the imbalance of the greenhouse gases. Four years later, 165 nations signed an international treaty, the United Nations Framework Convention on Climate Change. Some have compared it to the day in 1962 when Rachel Carson released her book, *Silent Spring*, in which she exposed the effect industrial greed was having on the environment. In particular she had discussed the effect of DDT on the world's food supply, which caused genetic damage to both animals and human beings.

The 1960s had awakened the Christian world to their responsibility to care for God's creation. As have seen, the environmental issue had become a religious issue with Lynn White Jr's article in which he blamed Christianity for the ecological crisis. He said Christians were arrogant towards nature and believed they had a right to use creation for their own benefit, a view first emphasized by Aristotle. Sadly, White's argument was partially true. Francis Schaeffer in *Pollution and the Death of Man* (1970) quoted this article in full in the appendix. White suggested Francis of Assisi's humble relationship with nature as an alternative and proposed that Francis of Assisi be a patron saint of ecologists.

Dr Rowan Williams, the former Archbishop of Canterbury, said, "The Christian reason for regarding ecology as a matter of justice ... is that God's self-sharing love is what animates every object and structure and situation in the world ... We are not consumers of what God has made; we are in communion with it."[62]

Apart from Francis Schaeffer's writings, however, evangelicals were slow to recognise their ethical responsibility to care for creation. In 1980 Calvin College, helped by a group of scholars, published, after three years of research, the first edition of *Earthkeeping: Stewardship of Creation*. Among the contributing scholars, two were well-known to me. They were Calvin De Witt, professor of Environmental Studies as the University of Wisconsin and the director of Au Sable Institute of Environmental Studies, and Dr

---

[62]   Rowan Williamson in the foreword for *Sharing God's Planet: a Christian Vision for a Sustainable Future* (London: Church House Publishing, 2005), p. vii.

Loren Wilkinson, at that time of Seattle Pacific College but later professor of Interdisciplinary Studies at Regent College, Vancouver. All the contributors to the publication were Americans. A revised edition was published in 1991 with 20 valuable articles.

The 1960s and 70s saw a theological divide between ecumenicals related to the World Council of Churches, and evangelicals related to the World Evangelical Fellowship and the Lausanne movement. In general, evangelicals have lagged several years behind the more ecumenical scholars on environmental issues.

Ecumenical institutions

The WCC, founded in 1948, brought together 160 Protestant and Eastern Orthodox churches. Its founding director, Dr Willem Visser 't Hooft, author of No Other Name (London: SCM, 1963), was sympathetic to evangelical theology, but as an ecumenical he was more committed to Christian unity. However, progressively the leadership of the WCC became strongly liberal in theology and critical of evangelicalism. In recent years the Theological Education Fund (TEF), a theological arm of the WCC, endorsed the Third Mandate period, 1970-1977, emphasizing contextualization. In 1970 TEF allocated $3.3 million to theological scholarships and library development, mainly to liberal seminaries in Asia, Africa and Latin America. "Contextualization" became the in word.

The Salvation Today conference in Bangkok in December 1972 focused on salvation in terms of liberating humankind from poverty, economic injustice and political exploitation. During this era the ecumenical movement focused on justice for people and little on justice for the environment. The ecumenical leadership in Asia was led by Kosuke Koyama, Song Chen-Chen, Lee Jong-Yong and Stanley Samartha. They developed their own national theological associations and were financially supported by the WCC. Paul Tillich was one western theologian favourably received by Asian ecumenicals.

The ecumenical approach since the 1960s has been to secularize creation so that the growth of the economy becomes the primary concern of both religious and political movements. The WCC Third Assembly in New Delhi in 1961 stated "The Christian should welcome scientific discoveries as new steps in man's dominion over nature."[63] The secularizing of

---

[63] From the New Delhi Report (London: SCM, 1962), 96. cited by Wesley Granberg-Michaelson in Eco-Theology, ed. David G. Hallman (Maryknoll, NY: Orbis Books, 1994), p. 97.

creation gave liberal theologians the opportunity to focus their theology on the social and political abuse of nature and the need for revolution to correct it.

By the WCC Assembly in Nairobi in 1975, the leaders were offering a critique of the prevailing growth philosophy and discussing the need for a "Just, Participatory and Sustainable Society" (JPSS). The issue now became the need for stability in both human and natural development. The WCC sub-unit, Church and Society, at Bucharest in 1974, had introduced this need. They held that growth needed to be limited and affirmed that the earth's non-renewable resources were not limitless. By 1980 sustainable development had become the framework for the Brundtland Commission, which led to the Earth Summit in Rio de Janeiro in June 1992, known as the UN Conference on Environment and Development (UNCED).[64]

The sustainability of creation was now becoming a global issue. This became evident in the WCC's sixth Assembly in Vancouver in 1984 where "the integrity of creation" became the linchpin of the ecumenical vocabulary. It was defined in terms of the interrelationship of justice and peace. Justice was seen as the starting point for the *Justice, Peace and Integrity of Creation* (JPIC) process.[65]

The leadership of the WCC on environmental issues continued to be set by the Church and Society sub-unit of the WCC and by the JPIC movement. At a consultation in Kuala Lumpur, Malaysia, in 1990 the JPIC stated: "The Spirit is God's uncreated energy alive throughout creation. All creation lives and moves and has its being in this divine life ... We also repudiate the hard lines drawn between animate and inanimate, and human and non-human. All alike and altogether in the bundle of life are groaning in the travail."[66]

This debate came to a conclusion at the JPIC convocation in Seoul in 1990, where the threat of global warming and climate change had become the key issues for future action. But the ecumenical leaders were unwilling to distinguish between the uniqueness of humanity, created in the image of God, and the creation of the rest of life. All of life was seen as one continuum. The evangelicals present protested, but to no avail.

The conflict over the relationship of humanity to the rest of created life became a major crisis at the 7th General Assembly in Canberra in 1991. Dr Chung Hyun Kyung of Seoul, South Korea, a Presbyterian lay theologian,

---

[64] Hallman, pp. 97-99.
[65] Ibid., p. 98.
[66] Report, *Church and Society*, Kuala Lumpur 1990, cited by Granberg-Michaelson, p. 100.

was invited to give a plenary session on the theme of the Assembly, "Come, Holy Spirit, Renew the Whole of Creation." Through music and pagan dance, she welcomed the oppressed spirits of the biblical past and the spirits of the underworld (including the pagan goddess of compassion) to be present. Protests came from the Orthodox Church members and from the evangelicals, of whom I was one. Dr Bong Ro and I later published a refutation of her presentation.[67] This incident further widened the gap between the ecumenicals and the evangelicals.

Against this radical background, it is inevitable that the Rio de Janeiro Earth Summit took a liberal approach to the issues of global warming. This continued to be the central concern of the Paris Agreement of 2015 where 187 countries were represented and most signed the Paris Accord. This document appealed to all governments and economic agencies to limit the rise of global temperatures to 1.5 degrees C. by 2050, by achieving zero growth of carbon dioxide and other gases. They feared 2050 to be a tipping point.

In contemporary scholarship the key issue is the relationship between the rising levels of CO_2 and global temperatures. A small number of scientists believe there is little or no connection between the two, while the IPCC scientists believe that rising CO_2 is the primary cause for the rise in global temperatures. Some climate sceptics have argued that the rise in global temperature is primarily the result of cyclic changes in the sun's radiation, aided by an increase in volcanic activity and the warming of the oceans resulting in cloud density from the increase in water vapour.

Indeed, the rising level of carbon dioxide may be due more to human greed, the striving for limitless economic growth, the increasing global population and to urban poverty. To what extent can political action control the burning of fossil fuels?

The relationship between the rise in global temperatures and the rise in global carbon dioxide continues to be debated by scientists, politicians and those with religious convictions. Nevertheless, the WCC ecumenical leaders commended the Paris Accord for taking into account the immediate needs of the poor countries most severely affected by extreme weather, although few of the poorer countries have been willing to pay the price of drastically reducing their level of economic development in order to limit the greenhouse gases. In fact, none have done so in spite of their promises made at the Paris Agreement.

In recent years the membership of the WCC has grown to 350 churches, including Pentecostal churches. It has become more theologically conser-

[67]   Bong Ro and Bruce Nicholls, *Beyond Creation*, Oxford, Regnum, 1992).

vative but continues to be dedicated to a search for the visible unity of the Church, to promote a common witness to mission and evangelism, to seek justice and peace and to uphold the integrity of creation. Its tenth assembly was held in Busan, Korea, in 2013, with the message, "God of Life, lead us to justice and peace" continued the theme.

Evangelical institutions

In 1969 I was invited by the fourth General Assembly of the World Evangelical Fellowship in Switzerland to establish an international theological commission, which I did under the name of the Theological Assistance Programme. At the same time Dr Saphir Athyal had also been asked by the South East Asia Congress on Evangelism to form a theological commission. He did this in Singapore in 1970, becoming its chairman. In cooperation with the Theological Assistance Programme, TAP Asia as it was called became the Asia Theological Association (ATA) in 1974 and Dr Athyal of India continued as chairman. An Asian member board appointed, Dr Bong Rin Ro of Korea as the first General Secretary, a position he held for the next twenty years.

ATA's first task was to establish two research centres, one in Seoul, South Korea, known as ACTS, and one in New Delhi, known as the Theological Research And Communication Institute (TRACI).

In 1977 I was privileged to found for the WEF Theological Commission the journal known as the Evangelical Review of Theology, and was its editor for 21 years.

Today ATA has become the strongest theological movement in Asia, with 361 member colleges in more than 30 countries. It set up an accrediting body for degrees from BTh to PhD.

Evangelical scholars in Asia have always emphasized salvation but have given scant attention to the care of the environment. The impact of Rachel Carson, Lynn White and Francis Schaeffer on the ecological crisis was not felt in the 1970s and 80s. Nor did it impact ATA members during those early years.

Evangelical Christianity is a culture which emphasizes personal responsibility in decision-making. This is reflected in the large number of evangelical church denominations, independent churches, and independent seminaries and Bible schools across Asia.

Evangelicals give priority to the mission of the church. Of the widely-recognised Five Spheres of Mission, initially stated by the Anglican Consultative Council in 1984 and repeated in 1990, the first is evangelism, leading to church planting. For evangelicals this overshadows the other four spheres of mission. It is the common purpose of a wide range of cross-cultural mission agencies whose primary focus is world evangelization.

The second and third spheres of mission, namely "to teach, baptize and nurture new believers" and "to respond to human needs through loving service," follow directly from this priority of evangelism. Relief and Development agencies such as World Vision, Tearfund and the Commission on World Relief share the same concerns, to reduce poverty and promote healthy and sustainable lifestyles. These concerns dominate relief and development programs in Asia, Latin America and the Caribbean. Then there are church bodies, especially the Salvation Army, the Methodist and Mennonite churches, and agencies such as City Missions, which seek to integrate these three spheres of mission.

It is significant that ecumenical agencies give greater priority than evangelicals to the fourth and fifth spheres of mission, namely to transform the unjust structures of society, to strive to safeguard the integrity of creation, and to sustain and renew the life of the earth.

In practice the integration of all five spheres of mission is essential to renew creation. I grieve that I know of few local evangelical churches and their mission agencies which give equal weight to all five spheres. To actively engage in mission, ecumenical and evangelical churches need to listen to each other.

Evangelicalism is a culture which differs in many aspects from ecumenical culture. I suggest seven distinctives of evangelical theology that shape their culture:

Individualism

Evangelicals give greater emphasis to personal freedom in decision-making than to the communal freedom more common with ecumenicals. Environmental issues become more personal than communal. This individualism is strongest among independent and charismatic/Pentecostal churches.

Mission as evangelism

Evangelicals give more priority to evangelism and church growth and less to justice in society and the care of creation. This applies to local and independent churches as well as global organisations such as the Lausanne Consultation on World Evangelisation (LCWE) 1974. As we have seen, evangelical relief and development agencies emphasise the need to reduce poverty and promote sustainable lifestyles—all within the context of evangelism.

The Authority of Scripture

Evangelicals give priority to the Bible, its inspiration, truthfulness and authority as the Word of God written. They believe that the Holy Spirit who inspired the biblical writers now illumines the minds of all who read the Scriptures in good faith and are willing to submit to its authority.

Conversion

The person and work of Jesus Christ is the centre of evangelical belief and practice. This is seen in their emphasis on the need for conversion, which is God's transforming work in the life of persons, leading them to turn from self-centred and sinful lifestyles and put their trust in Christ. Conversion signifies a commitment to union with Christ as Saviour and Lord, symbolised in baptism. It is often described as "being born again" after the words of Jesus' conversation with Nicodemus in John 3:3-7. To be converted is to become a disciple of Jesus.

Christ's Return to Earth

A unifying factor among evangelicals is the conviction that God, the creator of all things, loves his world and intends to restore and redeem it. They emphasise that the reign of the kingdom of God began when Jesus came to earth and will be consummated when Jesus returns to it as judge and redeemer.

Simple Lifestyles

Most evangelicals, but sadly not all, strive to live a simpler lifestyle and to overcome the craving for constant economic growth. They seek to reduce the gap between rich and poor by supporting the many mission and development agencies who are seeking to raise the general standard of living of the poor. They are called "to live more simply so that others may simply live." However, a large number of conservative evangelicals interpret 2 Peter 3:10 as saying that the earth and everything in it will be burned up. From this they conclude that evangelism and church planting must take almost exclusive priority over all other aspects of mission.

Stewardship of Creation

Evangelicals emphasise the second coming of Christ to earth as redeemer and Judge and in the light of this accept their responsibility to be faithful stewards of God's world. They recognise the importance of both human and non-human factors in climate change, but tend to be sceptical about the ability of governments to reverse climate change through carbon policies alone. They appeal to governments and people to adapt to the changes they cannot control.

Evangelical Institutions Committed to the Care of Creation

The Mission and Public Affairs Council of the Anglican Communion published *Sharing God's Planet: a Christian Vision for a Sustainable Future.* (2005) The authors describe the human abuses of creation and call upon God's people to share their own space with the rest of God's creation and to exercise dominion over it under God's rule. We are to enjoy earth's resources without jeopardizing future generations. The authors argue that after a century of growth without limit, we are now facing sudden changes in weather systems that demand a global response. They fear the earth could reach a "tipping point" whose consequences could be devastating.[68]

The writers also list a number of environmental organizations and websites in the UK that are church-based or church-related. I will mention three of them:

The Environmental Issues Network

This was set up in 1990 to link churches and agencies in the UK, to promote ecumenical cooperation and to avoid wasteful duplication. Professor R J Berry was the first chairman.

The John Ray Initiative

This is an educational charity with the twin themes of sustainable development and environmental stewardship. It was established in the UK in 1997 and named after the naturalist and theologian, John Ray (1627-1705).

---

[68] *A Report from the Mission and Public Affairs Council of the Anglican Communion* (London: Church House Publishing, 2005), p. 15.

A Rocha

Meaning "the rock" in Portuguese, A Rocha is an agency which seeks, alongside others, to respond to a world that produces two million tonnes of rubbish every day. This forum helps churches to show the relevance of the Christian faith on environmental issues and to care for creation in practical ways. A Rocha was founded in 1983 as a charitable society, and is now registered in the UK. It has a special concern to restore wetlands and birdlife, eliminate rodents from the forests, and sustain biodiversity[69] as it seeks to conserve and restore the habitat and its fauna and flora in 20 countries. I had the privilege of visiting their wetlands project in the Bakaa Valley in Lebanon.

Peter Harris, the founder and international coordinator, emphasises that God reveals himself in creation as well as in his saving revelation recorded in Scripture. The Lord loves and heals his creation.

Relief and Development Agencies

Many evangelical churches and mission agencies have their own relief and development agencies and are well-known for their leadership of global agencies including World Vision, Tearfund, World Relief Commission (USA) and Barnabas Fund. Each agency emphasises conversion and discipleship, pastoral care, compassion for all who suffer, and justice in society.

World Evangelical Alliance

The Evangelical Alliance was founded in 1846 in London, partly as a response to the emerging liberalism of the churches. It ceased to function after World War I, when liberal religion was no longer dominant.

Then in 1951 its successor, the World Evangelical Fellowship was founded in Woudschoten, the Netherlands. It brought evangelicals together to promote biblical belief, worship and mission, with a common goal: to disciple the nations for Christ. The Fellowship was rooted in historical biblical Christianity as practised throughout church history. It differed from the World Council of Churches (WCC) founded in 1948, also in the Netherlands, in its theology and its emphasis on individuals and

---

[69] See Stella Simiyu and Peter Harris, *Caring for Creation* (Cambridge, Grove Books, 2008) 2-28, for a broad survey of the need for environmental conservation and human responsibility.

institutions rather than the ecumenical unity of the churches as promoted by the WCC.

In 2002, WEF changed its name to the World Evangelical Alliance (WEA) but with the same Statement of Faith and ministry goals. WEA brings together 130 regional and national Evangelical Alliances/Fellowships in 123 countries. The Alliance sponsors commissions on theology, missions, women, youth, information technology, relief and development and religious liberty. The last two seek practical ways to care for creation and achieve justice in society and nature.

The Lausanne Committee for World Evangelization (LCWE)

Initiated by Billy Graham, LCWE grew out of a global conference held in Lausanne, Switzerland in July 1974, with 2700 participants. Each member present was invited to sign a document known as the Lausanne Covenant, prepared under the direction of John Stott. In fifteen paragraphs, the covenant called on Christians to critique their cultures (para 10), to engage in spiritual warfare against evil (para 11), and to secure peace, justice and liberty (para 13). While the movement has focused sharply on evangelization, it made little attempt to relate to the environmental issues which the WCC was already addressing.

The Manila Manifesto of the Second LCWE Congress in 1979 focused on evangelism, but again had virtually no reference to environmental issues. The Third Congress, in Cape Town (2010), thirty-one years later, maintained the same LCWE principles of "the whole church taking the whole gospel to the whole world." But for the first time, the "whole world" included both humanity and the natural world. It stated: "Since Jesus is Lord of all the earth, we cannot separate our relationship to Christ from how we act in relationship to the earth ... Such love for God's creation demands that we repent of our part in the destruction, waste and pollution of the earth's resources, and of our collusion in the toxic idolatry of consumerism."[70] The Cape Town Commitment of 2010 pointed to climate change as an urgent issue (Part 2, Section 5).

From 16-21 March 2020, the Lausanne/WEA Global Campaign for Creation Care and the Gospel planned to host its 11th regional consultation in Romania, but because of the Covid-19 pandemic it had to be postponed. However, the Call for Action of the Jamaica Consultation (November 2012)

---

[70]   *The Cape Town Commitment: a Confession of Faith and a Call to Action* (the Lausanne Movement, 2001), p. 19.

has already launched an evangelical global campaign to combat climate change. Participants have included theologians, scientists, creation care practitioners, and church leaders, including pastors.

Langham Partnership

Langham Partnership is a global organisation founded by John Stott in 1974. It is a network of evangelical leaders who aim to strengthen the global church. Its function includes supporting Langham Scholars in their PhD studies (380 graduates so far), and Langham Literature, which sponsored the *South Asia Bible Commentary* (2015) Its 160 contributors are all Asian nationals. Other regional commentaries in preparation include those in Latin America, the Middle East and Eurasia. Langham Preaching trains preachers at all levels. The former director of Langham, Christopher Wright, published a monumental work, The Mission of God.[71]

Joint Consultations between WEA (formerly WEF) and LCWE

These include:

- *1978 Gospel and Culture*, a consultation in Bermuda, led by John Stott. This was the first evangelical conference to respond to the issues of culture.
- *1980 An Evangelical Commitment to the Simple Life*, led by Dr Ron Sider of the Ethics unit of WEF. This was the first evangelical attempt in the modern era to respond to social injustices in society including poverty and excessive wealth.
- *1982 The Relationship between Evangelism and Social Responsibility (CRESR)*, a consultation led by John Stott and Bruce Nicholls which brought Word and deed together.[72]
- *1983 The Wheaton Consultation on the Nature and Mission of the Church* initiated by Bruce Nicholls. This had a third section devoted to the church's response to human need.

---

[71] Christopher J H Wright, *The Mission of God* (Nottingham: Inter-Varsity Press, 2006), 581 pp.
[72] Bruce J Nicholls, ed. *In Word and Deed* (Exeter, Paternoster Press, 1985).

Since then, the Langham Partnership has given strong leadership in the financing of theological scholars and sponsoring consultations on issues of national importance.

Leadership in the Developing World

Much of the development of evangelical theology and theological education and the contextualizing of national cultures has been led by autonomous bodies in Asia, Africa, Latin America and the Caribbean and by individuals.

The Asia Theological Association has convened many regional and national consultations, but has given little attention to environmental issues or climate change. Bong Ro has been succeeded by a number of able Asians, namely, Ken Gnanakan of India, Derek Tan of Singapore, Joseph Shao of the Philippines and now Theresa Lua, also of the Philippines. Similar associations have been formed in Africa, the Caribbean and Latin America.

Individual Asian Leaders

Much of the present engagement with environmental issues in Asia has come from individual leaders rather than from consultations. I mention six Asians with evangelical convictions. There are many others worthy of naming.

- *Hwa Yung* is an ecumenical theologian and bishop whose book, *Mangoes or Bananas* (1997) was widely received.
- **Simon Chan** wrote *Grass Roots Asian Theology: Thinking the Faith from the Ground Up* (2014) which breaks new ground in contextualizing theology in Asian cultures.
- *Lawrence Ko*, also of Singapore, the founder of the Singapore Centre For Global Mission (SCGM), is noted for his frequent planting of trees in the deserts of Mongolia. He describes this in his book, *Can the Deserts be Green?* (2014)
- *Vinay Samuel*, wrote *The Church in Response to Human Need* (1987), one of his many in which he dealt with social and environmental issues in Asia.
- **Ken Gnanakan**, who wrote *Responsible Stewardship of God's Creation* (2004), was the evangelical leader on environmental issues in Asia. He published many books on current environmental issues.

- *Vishal Mangalwadi*, who wrote *Truth and Transformation* (2009) is a severe critic of western culture and calls for the healing of the nations.
- *Vinoth Ramachandra*, of Sri Lanka, who wrote *The Recovery of Mission* (1996) appeals for Christ-centred salvation in the religious context of Asia, and looks to the restoration of life as in the Garden of Eden.

Chapter 7: The Church's Role in Sustainable Development

The Brundtland Report of the World Commission for Environment and Development of 1987 said "Development meets the needs of the present generation without compromising the ability of future generations to meet their own needs."[73]

This is the common human concern of most people in all nations. It is the concern of the IPCC scientists, the environmentalists, the politicians, the sceptics who deny that carbon is the main cause of climate change, and of churches worldwide.

Sustainable development aims "to provide harmony among human beings and between humanity and nature."[74] This will include meeting the needs of the poor and applying educational, economic and technical resources to achieve this harmony. The challenge is to overcome the tension between the insatiable human desire for economic growth and the need to conserve the plant and animal species for future generations. What, then, is the role of the churches in this momentous task?

First, we will define the problem. The steady loss of global biodiversity is an indication that we are failing to reach this harmony. The current rate of extinction caused by human beings is estimated to be up to a thousand times higher than the natural extinction rate, and is expected to grow further in future years.[75] The worldwide tendency is to focus on economic growth rather than on conserving the environment, The history of economic Marxism in Russia and now in China points to the destructive influence of godless policies which have nationalized all the means of production and put the use of land under centralized government control. Collective ownership has resulted in a tremendous loss of productivity. These Marxist governments compensate by focussing on industrial development.

---

[73] Cited by Dr Neil W. Summerton, "Principles for Environmental Policies" (*Evangelical Review of Theology*, vol. 17, no. 2, April 1993) quoting from *Our Common Future: World Commission on Environment and Development* (Oxford: OUP, 1987), pp226-227. Dr Summerton at the time of writing was head of the Water Directorate in the Department of Environment, UK.
[74] Ibid., p. 227.
[75] Ghillean Prance, quoted by Dick Tripp in *Caring for Creation*, p. 22.

Environmental Principles of Sustainability

Dr Neil Summerton points to three principles to guide environmental policies in order to achieve sustainable development:

The precautionary principle

The government should not wait, because of the lack of scientific, economic and political certainty until environmental damage has occurred. Rather it should act on its limited knowledge and in response to public opinion. This is a risky policy but may sometimes be necessary. It is hoped that in each case rational thinking will prevail. However, religious pressures, political ideologies and greed may lead to irrational decision-making, with destructive consequences. An example of the lack of knowledge and balanced thinking is seen in the youth protests inspired by Greta Thunberg of Sweden. Youth are sometimes motivated by extreme fears and they call for actions that are unattainable. At the same time, they have a message people need to hear.

The preventionary principle

This aims to address potential pollution at its source by eliminating the production of present pollutants, whether on land or in the sea. The overuse of fertilisers designed to enhance grass growth can poison the soil and lead to the pollution of rivers and lakes. The felling of primal rainforests for economic profit, as in Brazil, Indonesia and Malaysia, followed by the "slash and burn" of the stubble must end. The loss of forests not only upsets the fine balance of carbon dioxide and oxygen essential for all life, but also results on the extinction of the natural flora and fauna.

The "polluter pays" principle

Advocated by the Paris Accord, this says that the polluter must be held responsible for the cost of defiling the environment. This is reasonable and needs greater implementation but it can lead to injustices. Where the polluters are slum dwellers, they cannot pay for the consequences of their actions such as the diseases caused by uncollected garbage and the lack of sanitation. In these cases it is the city councils who should pay for the results of the pollution, but they rarely do so. It is easier to blame individuals than corporations for their neglect of duty.

The Church's Moral Responsibility and Accountability

One of the challenges facing the global church is to take a lead in self-examination. I fear many churches are failing in this responsibility, but we praise God that there are many which are rising to the challenge.

We may ask, *Is the zero increase of carbon achievable?* Should the taxes raised from it be used only to support reforestation? Since it will take many years for actions taken now to effectively reduce the crisis, governments and churches also need to focus on how to adapt to the changing climate, and especially to the issue of rising sea levels. To answer these questions, we need to explore the areas in which the global church has responsibility. History shows that it is a mistake for the church *as an institution* to be politically involved. But as functioning church members, Christians ought to be involved. The impact of the Clapham Sect in London in the early 1800s is a good example of a small group of committed Christians forming a voluntary society in order to protest such social ills as slavery. They saw it abolished in 1833. Thus the functioning church is called is to be a moral and prophetic voice in society's wilderness of greed, bribery and corruption. Will not God hold both the institutional church and the functioning church accountable for their response? I think so

The prophets of the Old Testament constantly pointed to Israel's moral failures and corrupt practices. Jesus did the same and we must follow his example. We need to ask ourselves, as local churches and as denominational bodies how far we are accountable for our actions or lack of them? We need to recognise that the earth is our common home and the future home for all human beings and the natural world.

The days of Genesis 1 are of unstated length, but each represents as creative act of God.

On the third day of creation, as recorded in Genesis 1, God created the seedbearing plants, each after their own kind, and the trees bearing fruit from their seeds. On the fourth day God made the celestial bodies visible. On the fifth day he created the fish in the waters and the birds in the air. Then on the sixth day, he created both animals and human beings in the same period, to demonstrate their interdependence. The human race is totally dependent on tree, plants and the oceans for our oxygen, on plants and animals for our food, and on the rain for our drinking water. We have a common home which we need to share. We also have a common future, for on the final Judgment Day God will take to his heavenly home those who have demonstrated their accountability to both humanity and nature. The earth will be "laid bare" (as in 2 Peter 3:10, NIV) or "disclosed" (NRSV), cleansed of evil, and finally creation will be restored, perhaps to be comparable to the Garden of Eden. The harmony in the animal kingdom, as promised by Isaiah in 11:6-10, and 65:17-25, will be fulfilled (Rev 21-22).

The main unit of society, especially in Asia, is the family which is the basis of the larger units of tribe, caste and ethnicity. The nations which have survived political crises, revolutions and wars have been those with strong and stable families, such as China and India. This stability is seen in the emphasis placed on celebrating marriages, funerals and the birth of children. These ceremonies may last a week.

Animals as well as human beings are family-based. Each year I watch two sparrows returning to the same corner of the spouting in my neighbour's home. They mate, build their nest, lay their eggs, and hatch and feed their chicks by turn until they are able to fly away. The next spring the same two sparrows return and start another family. God is good, and everything he created is good, created after its own kind.

Nevertheless, our world is in deep trouble. It is groaning and frustrated from human abuse and longs for liberation (Romans 8:18-27). We human beings are also in trouble. Family life is disintegrating, and millions of immigrants and refugees are fleeing from the cruelty and violence of their own religious people. Birds and animals don't normally starve, but today thousands of human beings are dying of starvation.

The climate is disturbed. People are suffering from floods, droughts, cyclones and bushfires. During 2019-2020 in South Australia and across the western states of the USA, large areas of inhabited and uninhabited land were burned, along with animals, property and people.

In the midst of our suffering world, God has appointed the church as the family of God to be the stewards of his creation and to show people on earth how to live and to triumph over the changing climate.

Stewardship in the life of the church

Churches as global families are made up of multiple denominations and independent local congregations that vary considerably in doctrine, lifestyle, practices and social levels. They are stable insofar as they acknowledge that Jesus Christ is their Saviour and Lord, and they look to the Holy Spirit for guidance and empowerment. God entrusts great responsibility to those he knows will be good stewards.

Peter summarised the church as "a chosen people, a royal priesthood, a holy nation and a people belonging to God" (1 Peter 2:9). Paul called it "God's household" whose foundations are the prophets of the Old Testament and the apostles of the New, with Jesus Christ as the chief cornerstone (Ephesians 2:19-22). Thus, the New Testament writers speak of the church in several ways—a local congregation, a city-wide community, or the bride of Christ. The apostles saw the church not only as a living organism and a structured institution for worshipping, preaching the Word, celebrating the Eucharist and serving the needy, but also as God's agent for justice in society.

The idea of stewardship of God's creation is developed in detail in the Old Testament, in terms of rightly tilling the soil according to the sabbatical principle of leaving it fallow for one year in seven (Leviticus 25). In the New Testament the stewardship of nature is implied in our relationship to God and to the world in which he has placed us. There is no separation of body and spirit in our accountability to God. The manifold gifts of the Holy Spirit are for the building of fruitful relationships between individuals and communities living in a social harmony and in harmony with nature.

In today's increasingly secular society our care of creation is becoming an effective bridge to lead people to faith in Christ. I endorse the words of Dr Robert Frost: "When Christians take the earth seriously, people take the gospel seriously." This has proved true in Nepal and in north-east India, leading to their rapid church growth.

The Cost of our Stewardship

There is a cost, however, in being openly involved in the life of the church. It will include criticism and persecution. Christ chose not to avoid the Cross. He chose to remain silent during his trial first by the high priest and then by Pilate, the Roman governor who alone had the right to execute prisoners. Jesus was willing to suffer and die for the sake of freeing others, past, present and future, from the consequences of sin. Jesus warned his followers that they would be persecuted, not for doing wrong but simply for being his disciples.

It is significant that throughout the history of the church, waves of persecution have been followed by peaceful times of rapid church growth. In the present wave of persecution in the Middle East, large numbers of Muslims are turning to Christ. When peace comes, the church will multiply. The church in Nepal exploded in the years 2000 to 2015 during this period of rest from severe persecution. During the 2015 Nepal earthquake Christians responded by helping to rebuild houses and restore village life. Theological colleges in Kathmandu closed and the student went to the village to help with the rescue work. People responded by taking the gospel seriously and many became followers of Jesus.

Suffering also comes to those who stand by the truth in their scientific understanding of God's laws of nature. The death of Galileo is an example.

In our time, Professor R J Berry of London University has suffered much criticism because of his belief in miracles.

Jesus through the apostle John warned that those who destroyed the earth would themselves be destroyed (Revelation 11:20). Responsibility leads to accountability. Our concern is to know how far the global church is willing to make sacrifices to lead in the restoration of creation. The temptation is to leave it to governments to allocate millions of dollars to solve the present ecological crisis, or to leave it to extreme left-wing politicians to give the lead.

Undoubtedly our progress in scientific knowledge is an important factor in reducing the present destructive level of greenhouse gases. But should we look to science alone to reduce the rising levels of these gases, especially carbon dioxide and methane? Or is it an issue of our personal lifestyles? To live a simpler lifestyle, we need to depend more on the Holy Spirit.

Dr Rowan Williams, the former Archbishop of Canterbury, called for churches to give an account of the extent that they are engaged in sustaining the land, the air and the sea. God in his creative goodness replenishes his creation through seed time and harvest, year after year.[76] Williams suggests that to account for their stewardship and impact on the environment, churches should think in terms of "footprints." This term is now widely used in the management of the present ecological crisis. By "footprint" Williams meant the human impact on the stability of the earth and asked whether we as the church were sustaining the earth or steadily adding to its destruction. This included the management of the waste which we as families and communities have generated.

In July 2004 the Archbishop called the global church to undertake an audit of its green credentials. He initiated the project "Eco-Congregation" which offered a toolkit of suggestions by which churches could undertake an audit and then improve their ecological track record.[77] Indications are that many churches are using this toolkit. As part of it, some have developed their own recycling schemes. The support and fair trading of organic foods is another example. *The Sharing of God's Planet* calls for a sustainable development to cover all three aspects of universal wellbeing: social, economic and environmental. Sustainable development means "enjoying the

---

76   *Sharing God's Planet: a Christian vision for a sustainable future* published by the Mission and Public Affirms Council of the Church of England (London: Church House publishing, 2005), pp. 30-37.

77   Ibid., p. 34.

earth's resources without jeopardising future generations."[78] This is in line with Jesus' call to his disciples to be the salt of the earth and the light of the world (Matthew 5:13-16).

Pope John-Paul II with the Ecumenical Patriarch, Bartholomew I, in a pastoral letter titled "A Common Declaration on Ecumenical Ethics," said: "A solution at the economic and technological level can be found only if we undergo, in the most radical way, an inner change of heart which can lead to a change in lifestyle and of sustainable patterns of consumption and production. A genuine conversion in Christ will enable us to change the way we think and act."[79] We agree.

Since the issues of the present climate crisis are ultimately spiritual, a spiritual answer is needed to solve them. This begins with a radical change of heart. Churches are commissioned by Christ to be agents of compassion and justice in a broken world. They are called to identify with God's healing work of both people and animals.

Compassion and Justice in the Care of Creation

The most common entry point to faith is the demonstration of compassion to those who are suffering for whatever reason. In Nepal, as in other Asian countries, healing by faith, as well as the exorcism of evil spirits are major factors in conversions to Jesus Christ.

The concern of this chapter is to build relationships with other people who enjoy nature in order to share our enthusiasm for the beauty of creation, but also protest against abuse such as the killing rhinoceroses for their horns in order to smuggle their ivory out to China.

A central concern of both the Old and New Testaments is that God is holy and acts justly but with love and compassion for those who are suffering from the effects of natural disasters and human abuse. The Hebrew terms for justice and righteousness are interchangeable. They reflect the biblical concepts of law and grace and are central to God's covenant, first with Moses and then Isaiah and with Amos and Micah, and finally with Jesus for our benefit. Likewise, the Psalms pour forth God's message of both justice and compassion, as in Psalms 33:5-9, 82:3-4, 85:10-11, 103:13 and in 145:8-9.

---

[78] Ibid., p. 31.
[79] Pope John Paul II *Pastores Gregis*, para 70, cited in *Creation and Hope*, ed. by Nicola Hoggard Creegan and Andrew Shepherd (Eugene, OR: Pickwick Publications, 2018), p. 196.

In view of the escalating loss of biodiversity, the loss of natural forests and the pollution of our land, air and water resources, Christians and their churches need to be more vocal in their protests. We cannot just leave the rightful use of nature to extreme left-wing politicians or to politically-biased scientists. One good example is that the government of Nepal has refused to allow Monsanto, the producer of GMO seeds, to enter the country, in their concern to protect the freedom of the farmers to grow their own seed.

The future crisis that could lead to widespread war is not oil but water. Clean drinking water is the first priority in the modern world, since millions die each year from diseases caused by polluted water. Nations such as India and Pakistan live in constant tension over the control of their rivers which originate in the Indian Himalayas.

Justice and compassion are integral to God's healing of the land. Churches grow when evangelism and justice are seen as part of the same gospel. To build relationships based on environmental justice issues may be one way to introduce the claims of Jesus.

For the local church to have such an impact on other people, they must give evidence that they are a worshipping community of joyous praise, who love to hear the Scriptures faithfully expounded. They must also be a praying community as a local church and as families belonging to it. When we pray regularly for a person or a family, we begin to love them as never before and to identify with them in their needs. Through prayer the Holy Spirit creates a relationship of trust between Christians and those we pray for.

When we read the Psalms, we experience the joy of nature and praise for God the Creator. Psalms 8, 19, 96, 104, 107, 145, 146 and 148 give special recognition to the wonder of God both creating and sustaining his creation. Christians are encouraged to likewise praise him. Jesus too was a great lover of nature. He sometimes referred to the birds of the air who neither sowed nor reaped nor stored away in barns "and yet your heavenly Father feeds them." He referred to the lilies of the field: "Even Solomon in all his splendour was not dressed like one of these" (Matthew 6:26-29).

Jesus said, "If God clothes the grass of the field, which is here today and tomorrow is thrown into the fire, will he not much more clothe you, O people of little faith?" (Matthew 6:26-29). Three quarters of Jesus' parables were centred on lessons from nature. Our love for Christ must overflow with love for his creation, a love we want to share with others.

Against this background I want to discuss three steps in our church's relationship with God's creation, as suggested by Tripp and Bookless:

Dick Tripp used the alliterative words, reduce, reuse, recycle, resist, restore and rejoice to summarise the practical outworking of relationships between people with common environmental interests.[80] Dave Bookless presented a similar list: to reduce, reuse, recycle and refuse.[81]

Practical Applications of Sustainability

1. Living Simply

Our starting point must be to simplify our lifestyle, as in the slogan, "Live simply so that others can simply live." It is a tragedy that so many obese people, including children, are struggling to lose weight, while at least one-third of the world's people don't have enough to eat, and every year thousands die of starvation.

To live simply begins with eating less, including less red meat. According to the One Green Planet website, the United Nations Food and Agriculture Organization finds that beef production gives rise to more greenhouse gases than the transportation industry.[82]

Michael Mosley's bestseller, *Fast Diet*[83] is a helpful guide to a Mediterranean diet of fish, eggs and chicken for protein with plenty of vegetables, fruit and nuts. He suggests a one- or two-day a week partial diet of 600 calories based on a small breakfast and evening meal and no lunch. I can testify that this works. To reduce is to refuse to eat the foods we don't need. But to live simply also means having fewer clothes, fewer household gadgets, less unnecessary travel, and for some of us, fewer magazines and books! One of the pleasures of life is to generously support needy causes.

2. Recycling and Reusing

This is a positive challenge for both family life and local church practices. The present global campaign is to recycle plastic containers. Every minute, the equivalent of one full garbage truck of plastic trash is dumped in the sea. That is 1440 trucks per 24 hours and 8 billion kilos per year."[84] Plastics pollute the beaches, increase water acidity and kill the fish (especially

---

[80] Dick Tripp, *Caring For Creation*, pp. 123-124.
[81] Dave Bookless, *Planetwise*, pp. 122-123.
[82] https://www.onegreenplanet.org/animalsandnature/beef-production-is-killing-the-amazon-rainforest/.
[83] Michael Mosley and Mimi Spencer, *The Fast Diet*, 2013.
[84] https://www.plasticsoupfoundation.org/.

whales) which unknowingly ingest the plastic. Plastic is non-biodegradable and is a curse both on the land and in the oceans.

Some local churches sponsor collection bins for degradable and non-degradable refuse, and encourage their congregations to bring their refuse to the church bins. Some household goods including electronic items can be collected for recycling and restored for meaningful use. Many churches encourage their members to support "op shops" (thrift stores) by donating their reusable possessions. I worked with one church that had its own weekly op shop supported by several church members. It introduced many neighbours to the life of the congregation. It is good to remember that all our possessions are gifts from God and that we are accountable to him for their use.

Another entrance point to recycling and reusing is to maintain the cyclic Sabbath principle of rest from work one day in seven in order to honour the Creator. (In biblical times the principle was also observed one year in seven for the land to lie fallow.)

3. Restoring God's garden and rejoicing

In order to educate the congregation to the joy and health-giving activities of growing vegetables, plants and flowers, the local church can establish its own gardens. I am in touch with several churches that sponsor their own raised gardens alongside their church buildings. The smallest space can be turned into a model garden to provide seedlings for church members as well as fruit and vegetables. A member of the congregation who teaches compost making is contributing to our care for God's creation.

I am familiar with a local church in Singapore which has its own aviary and a rabbit hutch, much to the delight and education of the children.

The local church, no matter how small its property, should be a public testimony to our confidence in God as Creator. Our desire is to honour him with the upkeep of the property. An untidy church building belies the transforming power of the Gospel.

Churches can be encouraged to sponsor their own tramping clubs as an expression of their love for God's creation. I used to belong to one such church club that plans a monthly walk, usually of ten to fifteen kilometres, through forests, over green fields and along beaches. It was not only a health-giving exercise but also an opportunity to experience the wonder, beauty and order of God's creation. It attracted people of other faiths as well as those with no faith and was a wonderful chance to build bridges of mutual understanding.

Churches need to sponsor lectures on the care of creation. Potential guest speakers are readily available. Research centres are needed to explore both the plurality of cultures and the various environmental issues.

Then there are Christian nature care organizations that offer challenging programmes in tree planting and in pest control. As we have seen, A Rocha offers an outstanding introduction to the Christian care of creation.

We rejoice that "The earth is the Lord's and everything in it, the world and all who live in it" (Psalm 24:1). When we work with God in sustaining his creation we increasingly want to rejoice at its greatness and perfection.

Christians are especially privileged to be invited to be stewards of God's creation.

I was part of an environmental aid agency known as Farms India. We taught farmers how to increase their crops and how to market their crops when the price of rice or wheat was high. We also made small loans so poor Christians could begin their own businesses. We gave a loan to a widow to buy a buffalo. The daily sale of its milk was sufficient to meet her needs. We financed four-wheel carts so that unemployed Christians could hawk fruit or cloth around the suburban streets. We gave a sewing machine to a woman to enable her to begin a tailoring business. Loans were to be repaid when the businesses became profitable. Very few failed to repay their loans.

Is Climate Sustainability Possible?

The issue is: can we sustain our global economic growth and development and at the same time lessen climate extremes with their consequence of human suffering? Also, can we save our rainforests, biodiversity, and reduce the pollution of land, air, water and sea? My answer is yes and no.

No

Politicians, scientists and many Christian organization are working hard to keep the rise of global temperatures to 1.5 degrees C. above the level of what they were at the beginning of the Industrial Revolution. Otherwise, they fear a tipping point towards environmental disaster. They assume that by reducing the use of fossil fuels—coal, oil and gas and in particular the level of carbon dioxide in the air—they will slow down the rise of global temperatures.

As we have seen, a minority of scientists are sceptical, believing that CO_2 is a minor component of greenhouse gases and has little influence on climate change. They see other factors as more important. Moreover, they fear that the large amount of taxpayers' money being spent on controlling the level of CO_2 will detract from the nations' ability to cope with radical climatic changes such as floods and droughts.

The majority group are supported by wide publicity, while sceptics are kept on the fringe of the debate and given little public finance for their cause.

There is good evidence that the western world is making progress in their reduction of the use of fossil fuels, but they are a minority in the world's population. The global future will be determined by the nations of Asia, Africa and Latin America with their growing populations and increasing number of people living in poverty, but at present their contribution to controlling climate change is minimal. China and India, despite their efforts to control the use of fossil fuels, are the biggest polluters. Several of the polluting cities in Asia are larger than the populations of some western nations.

Then the addition of two billion people by 2050, most of whom will be living in the developing world, is going to increase pollution. The growing middle-class populations of these developing nations are demanding living standards comparable to the west, but this will inevitably contribute to the global problem. Above all, unless the human problems of greed, the lust for pleasure and power, and the widespread violence are controlled, the imbalances of the global climate will not be resolved.

While China is pioneering its electric car and solar and wind energy, its expanding industrial development is increasing pollution and the level of greenhouse gases. The global motor industry is a major producer of CO_2. The production of motor cars has risen to 92 million per year.[85] The hope of totally replacing them with electric vehicles is unrealistic.

President Xi Jinping of China's "belt and road initiative" (BRI) will certainly increase the level of carbon in each region. He is establishing Economic Zones (SEZs) as the road to progress across Asia, in order to build Chinese-controlled and staffed cities and expand Chinese industrial development. One such city is Khorgas, on the Chinese border with Kazakhstan, which now has a population of 200,000. The BRI will certainly increase the level of carbon in the region.

In September 2018 President Xi announced his long-term plan for China to be carbon neutral by 2060 by shifting the production of electricity from coal to wind power and solar panels. His short-term incentives are to

---

[85]   https://www.statista.com/statistics/262747/worldwide-automobile-production-since-2000/.

promote economic development until 2030. He lifted the ban on coal-burning plants.

Since China joined the Paris Agreement in 2015, China's coal consumption has steadily increased and steel mills dependent on coal have been expanded. Billions of dollars are being loaned to build coal-burning plants in developing countries.

In addition to these human factors, natural factors in climate change are beyond human control. The sun's influence on the earth is immense, being 100 times larger than the earth and having a temperature of 10,000 degrees at its surface. Any changes in the radiation of ultraviolet and other gases will directly affect the earth's temperature. Likewise, any changes of the earth's revolution around the sun will also directly influence the climate. So, the issue becomes whether or not the earth's climate is cyclic. Humanly speaking, therefore, my answer to the question of whether the future sustainability of the climate is possible is *no*.

Yes

From a Christian perspective, our answer is *yes*. God will hold us accountable for our care of his world. As human beings, we are responsible for the abuse of the environment, resulting in adverse climate change. We are responsible for the widening gap between rich and poor, global poverty and the growing shortage of clean drinking water. I will outline in the final chapter some of the actions we need to take.

Dr Ken Gnanakan in *Responsible Stewardship of Creation*, has a number of suggestions affirming eco-justice, the reduction of global poverty, debt reduction for poor nations and respect for the rights of indigenous people. He also calls for the building of national financial stability. Eco-justice needs to be taught in schools, and individual and church lifestyles need to recognise they are accountable both to God and to their nations.

From a divine perspective, our answer is also *yes*. As we have seen, the environmental problems are both spiritual and moral, and call for spiritual and moral answers. Christians assume the Bible is the revealed Word of God. We believe God is the Creator of all things, and that the earth, which is unique on our solar system, is the special sphere of his redeeming love. The Psalmist cries, "How many are your works, O Lord. In wisdom you made them all!" (Psalm 104:24).

God will not allow sinful human beings to destroy his world. He grieves over the human abuse of it, and chastises both Israel and Christians for their failure to keep his commandments. God's message to Israel was that he would heal the land if they were faithful to him, while his message to the church is that he will establish his kingdom on the whole of the earth, but only when the Gospel is known in every ethnic community will he return (Matthew 24:14). Then God in his justice and compassion will redeem creation,

As we have seen, prophecies such as Isaiah 11:6-9 point to God's ultimate re-creation and harmony of all of life, human and environmental., As stewards of his creation we are called to rule over it for good and to subdue its evils. We cannot love God and our neighbour without having care for God's creation, because the earth is our home which we share with all living beings, so we are called to be "healers" of a broken world, restoring God's glory to it.

To the question, *Is the future sustainability of the earth possible?* the answer is *yes*, but only if God does it and if we are faithful to him as co-workers and stewards of his land. He will hold the church community accountable for its compassion and commitment to meeting the needs of the people oppressed by human greed and suffering from unjust practices.

Chapter 8: How Then Shall We Live?

The issue of this chapter is, how shall we live well as part of the natural world to which we belong? The earth is our common home on which people depend for their daily food and oxygen, while nature depends on people and animals for carbon dioxide.

In modern times it is possible to go through life with little thought about the natural world we live in, except when the weather turns against us, such as when we have cyclones, droughts and fires. How then shall we live in a world of changing climates? We can either resist it in a spirit of helplessness or defiance, or determine to live well, by acts of the will, and by adapting to the changing as well as we can. Many who live in high-rise apartments in large cities have little or no contact with the world of nature, and little incentive to pause and enjoy it in wonder and praise. We will describe some better ways to live:

Enjoy our cultural heritage

South Asian cultures developed from the Indus Valley culture of 4500 years ago to the Aryan and Hindu cultures of north India, beginning between 4,000 and 3,500 years ago. Later came the Buddhist and Jain cultures, and then the Muslim culture of the last 1400 years and the Sikh culture of the last 500 years. Parallels are found in the Chinese cultures of Taoism, Confucianism, Buddhism and Japanese Shintoism.

Every culture is rich in beauty, creativity and goodness, and to be enjoyed. At the same time, it also has idolatrous and demonic practices, the consequence of human pride, greed and lust for power. Christian culture became distinctive when God made a covenant with Abraham 4000 years ago and later renewed it with Moses and then with David. Finally, God made a new covenant with the disciples of Jesus Christ. In each case the land influenced the direction of the culture, along with a range of historical, political, economic and social factors.

The art of living well depends on human ability to adapt to both cultural and environmental change. We recognise that no Christian practice is free from cultural influence, as seen in the plurality of our systematic theologies and our church denominations.

Christianity's strength is in the authority it gives to the Bible and the fundamental doctrines outlined in it. The basic issue in Asian religions is whether or not God is the creator of all things. Biblical faith claims that

God created the universe *ex nihilo*. This separates Christianity from the cultural religions of Hinduism and Buddhism which deny that the universe, including the earth, had a beginning.

The goal of the traditional Asian religions is to merge with God. Hindus think of the natural world as Mother Earth, being without beginning or end. They see the natural world as evolving from the Absolute, viewed either as personal or impersonal.

Some Christians believe that after the world was created by God, people were created immediately from dust. Other Christians view all of creation as the progressive act of God over long periods, from chaos to order and from inanimate to animate life, culminating in Adam and Eve as the high point of God's created order. In other words, they see a progressive development of life on earth, initiated and sustained by God himself. This gives meaning and purpose to creation. Science can analyse the timings and structures of this progress, but cannot explain its purpose or meaning. That depends of divine revelation.

Christianity and science are not in conflict. They each answer different questions. God's two books, revelation and nature, complement each other. Christians may accept some truths from evolutionary science, but vigorously oppose philosophical evolutionism which claims that the changes in nature are *sui generis*, purely internal to their organisation.

Biblical revelation is clear that God's purpose is to restore the creation that humankind has abused and is destroying. In his sermon following the healing of the crippled beggar, Peter, speaking of Christ as Lord said, "He must remain in heaven until the time comes for God to restore everything as he promised long ago through his holy prophets" (Acts 3:21). This restoration will only be complete when Christ returns to consummate his kingdom on earth. It is foolish to predict when this will happen, though Scripture does give some indication of how believers are to prepare for his coming. Christ exhorts his followers to pray and meditate, examine themselves, confess their sins and live by faith, empowered by the Holy Spirit.

For Christians, to enjoy their culture is to enjoy the gift of creativity as seen in the literary, music and art forms found in it. It also means to enjoy the satisfaction of clear, rational thinking, reaching answers to life's uncertainties.

The complexity and extent of human languages reflects differences in cultures.

Then these gifts of creativity find their human enjoyment in the beauty, colour, shapes and smells of flowers, in the grandeur of the snowy mountains, and the timeless flow of the tides. We marvel at the harmony and interdependence of each form of life in nature. The book of

Ecclesiastes captures both the meaninglessness of life and the wisdom of God's works. God has put an awareness of eternity in the hearts of all people, "yet they cannot fathom what he has done from the beginning to the end" (Ecclesiastes 3:11). The cultural plurality of the writers of the Psalms is a reminder of God's love and faithfulness through all generations. The Psalmist says "He forgives all your sins and heals all your diseases. He redeems your life from death and crowns you with love and compassion" (Psalm 103:3-4). We cry with the Psalmist, "O Lord, how majestic is your name in all the earth" (Psalm 8:1).

I will never forget the awe of standing 10,000 feet up in a wide field of minute mountain flowers in the Himalayan foothills. The wonder at God's creativity was overwhelming.

At the same time, God is holy and just. He destroys evil in its many manifestations. His judgment on his own people for their sins was severe. In our present affluent societies, we need God to send more prophets like Amos to warn of God's judgment on human corruption.

But the overall picture is that of God sustaining and restoring his creation, to his everlasting glory. The biblical story began with Adam and Eve taking care of the Garden of Eden and ends with the River of Life flowing from the throne of God with the leaves of the trees on either side of the river designed for "the healing of the nations" (Revelation 22:2).

Transform our culture to reflect the culture of Jesus

Jesus is the Christian's model of one who transformed his natural culture to the glory of God his Father. Jesus was born about 4 BC, in a village of Palestine. His mother Mary was a village girl, and his adoptive father a carpenter by trade. He would have gone to the local synagogue school, spoken Aramaic and Hebrew, and possibly some Greek or Latin since the Romans were the political rulers. In this way Jesus identified with his Hebrew culture and its educational system. He grew up to know and love his Hebrew scriptures. He also identified with and loved nature, as seen from all his parables.

He was conscious from his boyhood, however, that he belonged to another culture, one which he identified as the kingdom of God. In his teaching he emphasized two distinct but related spheres of this kingdom – complete love and loyalty to God and unlimited love for one's neighbour.

Then from his baptism he entered into conflict with the demonic powers that were controlling nature. He exorcised evil spirits from both men and women, and promised the eventual destruction of Satan and his angels. He warned that Satan was active as "a wolf in sheep's clothing." At the same time Jesus liberated the people he met who were suffering from sickness and disease, the deaf and the blind. He mourned with those who were suffering bereavement, he accepted the suffering and death of the cross as the will of his heavenly Father, and in rising from the dead he broke the bonds of death and satanic power.

His resurrection was the beginning of a new order of creation, for he was both God and man. To the amazement of his disciples he ascended to heaven, taking the marks of his suffering with him.

From the beginning of his ministry Jesus was conscious that he had been sent from God his Father, as the promised Messiah to the Jewish community, and as the Son of God to the whole world. At the Last Supper he told them that the Holy Spirit would come in his place to lead them into all truth. In the Garden of Gethsemane, he fully accepted the Father's will for his atoning death. Throughout his ministry he had one message: the coming of the kingdom of God. He called people to enter this kingdom and to accept him as their king. In demanding total allegiance from his followers, Jesus set a path for moral and spiritual freedom that they had never known.

In his brief life Jesus transformed his Jewish culture to become the culture of the kingdom of God. He can do the same today. Only those who accept his kingly rule as Lord are freed from the legalistic bonds of their traditional cultures. He said, "For if the Son makes you free, you shall be free indeed" (John 8:36). Society punishes people by taking away their freedom. They are put in prison, in some cases for life. God will punish evildoers on the Day of Judgement.

How then should we live in today's world with its many cultures, especially in Asia? Nepal, for instance, has many religious and ethnic heritages, and its people must live together peaceably. The ethnic background includes the early Dravidian Indians, the Indo-Aryans, the Tibetan-Burmans and the animist tribals.

Over its 4500 to 5000 years of religious history, Nepal has assimilated many religious traditions and seen many different political regimes. Hinduism is the dominant religion, followed by Buddhism which is often merged with Hindu culture and temple practices. There are also more than a million Muslims, representing 4.4 percent of the population, as well as a growing Christian community from 1960 who need to adapt their traditional cultures to the culture of the kingdom of God.

Singapore is another country with interreligious harmony. There every effort is made to control all extremist communities. Buddhist Chinese see China as their homeland, Muslim Malays look to Malaysia, Hindu Indians to India and Christians look to many cultures.

Live More Simply

The increased mental stress in today's world is a sign of our failure to live more simply.

To live well in today's society begins with taking care of our bodies. As human beings we cannot live without food which the sea and land provide. We depend on the biblical principle of each living creature reproducing "after its kind." This means that physical death is part of the mercy of God so that life can continue to prosper.

To live well is also to have a plentiful supply of fresh, drinkable water. Planet Earth is unique in its abundance of it.

To live well also calls for a balanced diet. A good supply of fresh vegetables, fruit and nuts are essential for a healthy diet. Not everyone realises that the care of the stomach is essential to a healthy heart and active brain.

While red meat is permitted, today it needs to be eaten in moderation for good health. In the healthy Mediterranean diet, red meat is excluded, but one of the tragedies in today's world is that the primal rain forests, especially in the Amazon basin of Brazil, are being destroyed for grasslands in order to raise beef for the rich western market. Further, the rainforest countries such as in Indonesia and Malaysia are being replaced by palm plantations for the production of the more profitable palm olive oil.

The exploitation of the chicken industry is a blot on modern society. Hens are bred in cages and force-fed for their meat and eggs. Those who love nature and good health campaign for the production of only free-range eggs and chicken meat. The only sure foods are organically grown but more expensive.

Added to good food is the need for regular daily exercise. Walking is the best form, although running for short lengths also stimulates good health. Healthy sports at all ages also contribute to purposeful living, as does adequate daily rest.

Another side to living well is to be at peace both with God and with one's family and neighbours. A relationship with God is necessary if we are to have a good relationship with our neighbours.

Dr Ken Gnanakan, whose home is a testimony to simple living, rightly emphasizes that "establishing right relationships is the key to resolving our environmental crisis."[86]

In the Creation story God entrusted the first human beings with the impressive responsibility to be stewards of all that he had created, to rule

---

[86] Ken Gnanakan, *Responsible Stewardship of God's Creation* (Bonn, World Evangelical Alliance, 2014), p. 80.

over all that was good in creation, and to subdue all that was evil. The biblical message is that we cannot do all this in our own strength. We are dependent on God to help us. But responsibility always carries accountability, and this is where many Christians fail. Accountability leads to both judgment and reward. God is both loving and righteous in all his acts. Judgement and hope are the recurring message of the Bible.

Guard the Integrity of Creation

Clause 5 of the Mission Statement of the global Anglican Communion states our environmental responsibility as "to strive to safeguard the integrity of creation and to sustain and renew the life of the earth."

Challenge Ideological Misunderstandings

Before going into detail on this point it is helpful to review two ideologies which misunderstand this responsibility or give only a partial response to it.

Deep Ecology

In 1972 Arbe Naess founded the Deep Ecology movement, calling for a deeper and closer identification with all of nature, without any philosophical or religious assumptions. Deep Ecology seeks to evaluate nature in itself without any religious connotation. Non-theistic Buddhists are able to identify with this movement. From a Christian perspective, experience is not an adequate reason for safeguarding the integrity of creation. It needs a sense of purpose to motivate it.

In its support, Gnanakan notes that Deep Ecology has given rise to the Animal Rights movement, which many Christians now espouse.[87] The appalling loss of biodiversity is challenging us to take more seriously the rights of animals and birds. In the past it was Christians who gave leadership in the care of animals. The stories about Francis of Assisi caring for animals and birds are well known The Royal Society for the Prevention of Cruelty to Animals was founded by evangelical clergy, inspired by William Wilberforce.

---

[87]   Ibid., p. 75.

Eco-feminism

In 1975 Rosemary Ruether, author of the first eco-feminist book, New Woman/New Earth,[88] called for the end of patriarchy which saw men as responsible for the destruction of the earth. She claimed that women because of their reproductive ability have a strong relationship to nature. This qualifies them to have the leadership role in the care of creation. She blamed western male leaders for devaluing both women and nature. She criticised the biblical story for advocating male leadership which had led to the abuse of creation, and argued that in order to sustain a healthy ecological culture and society "we must transform relationships of domination and exploitation into relationships of mutual support."[89] Rosemary Ruether's chapter on "Ecofeminism and Theology" (p 199-204) is an excellent summary of her views.

Evangelicals, while not accepting Ruether's theological assumptions, recognise her contribution to justice in society and in nature. Moreover, all evangelicals should critique their own interpretation of Scripture and its consequence for the world of nature.

Sustain and renew the life of the earth

As we have seen, God's first mandate to the humankind he had created was "Be fruitful and increase in number; fill the earth and subdue it. Rule over the fish of the sea and the birds of the air and every living creature that moves on the ground" (Genesis 1:28). To "subdue" can mean either to take charge of it or to subdue the consequences of evil that were about to enter the world. To *rule* and to *manage* is the responsibility of a steward, a concept that is widely used in Scripture for our responsibility over the whole of creation. We endorse the World Council of Churches' call for "a just, participatory and sustainable society." As stewards of creation, we are called to bring together the church, creation and whole community under the lordship of the triune God in order to both rule and subdue his world.

On the Day of Judgment, we will be held accountable for our use of earth's resources, of which the most important is the availability of clean drinking water. It is as much a human right as food. No one can live for

---

88   Rosemary Ruether, *New Woman New Earth, Sexist Ideologies and Human Liberation* (NY, Seabury Press, 1975).
89   *Ecotheology: Voices from South and North*, ed. David G. Hallman (Maryknoll, NY, Orbis Books, 1994) 204.

more than a few days without water. Closely linked with it is the need for sanitation, grossly unavailable in the slums of our Asian cities.

Other natural resources which are steadily declining are the primal forests, with their birds and the insects. However, while people are dying painfully from starvation and the consequences of extreme weather conditions, birds and animals also die but in a less severe way. Normally they can cope better with climatic extremes.

To sustain the life of the planet, human beings need to adapt to its changes.

As we have mentioned earlier, the slow but steady rise of sea levels as glacial ice melts at the poles and in the Himalayas may become a serious problem to coastal cities before the end of the 21st century. This is now at crisis level for several islands in the Pacific which face the submersion of their island homes.

The renewal of creation needs to go beyond sustaining it if the mandate given first to Noah is to be fulfilled. However, the greater challenge to both sustaining and renewing the earth is the steady increase in immorality. Human beings are failing in this mandate because of human sin, expressed in greed for all that money can buy, in sexual abuse and the loss of human dignity, and in the striving to control other people.

In the end, however, it is nature that suffers the most. Political leaders who are self-seeking and dictatorial are the ones who most manipulate the natural world. Extremists create terrorism and wars resulting in enormous loss of human life and the degradation of the environment, as we have seen in the present regimes of China and North Korea and in the Marxist rule of Russia where millions died and natural resources were destroyed.

Despite the growth of an economic middle class in many developing nations, poverty is increasing as the world's population increases. The growth of megacities means natural resources are overstretched to provide necessities for their inhabitants. Added to this are the millions of refugees fleeing from oppressive countries for a freer life, mostly in the Christian west. The rich Muslim nations have selfishly closed their doors to refugees.

The rapid development of technology has both aided and negated the renewal of society and of creation. The electronic media have greatly enriched human culture. Digital technology has enabled online education, families to stay in contact, and businesses to be run from home. Despite the pandemic shut-down, social and religious institutions have been able to conduct their meetings online. Likewise, Asia-wide prayer meetings are being held. However, modern digital technology also has a negative impact. The easy availability of pornography has become a major moral problem. Gambling and illicit drugs have also become readily available, resulting in violence. The TV media enable politicians to influence election results, and constant advertising turns needs into wants.

Adapt to Change

Over the centuries people have learned how to adapt to their changing environment. Globally, we have experienced extremes in our weather—natural and regional droughts, forest fires, cyclic floods, volcanic explosions, earthquakes and tsunamis.

An example of a nation developing its own plans to adapt to climate change is Bangladesh, where they have developed an early warning system allowing people to evacuate to concrete cyclone shelters. They are building sea walls to protect low-lying coastlands. Bangladesh's cyclone death toll has been dropping for several decades, but capital is needed.[90] The UN Framework Convention on Climate Change has set up a Green Climate Fund to enable developing countries to develop their own adaptation plans.

We must now adapt our resources in order to cope with many diseases, pestilences and pandemics, which have been escalating over the past fifty years.

With rising sea levels, the Pacific Island atolls are one example where adaptation is becoming less easy. The islanders are having to look for new national homes.

Western nations, and the richer ones of the developing world such as Japan, are allocating vast financial resources to meet the Paris Agreement appeal in order to reduce the use of fossil fuels of coal and oil. They may reduce the amount of carbon they produce, but globally few nations are willing to accept simpler lifestyles. There has been a rapid population growth in the poorer nations of Asia, Africa and Latin America, and the emerging middle class in these nations is demanding more material resources. This, along with the growth of all megacities, inevitably increases global pollution. The growth of global transport on land, air and sea, the continuing deforestation and the failure to reduce the use of pesticides, suggests the difficulty if not impossibility of reaching zero carbon by 2050.

The call to safeguard the environment begins with true and faithful worship.

---

[90]   *The Economist*, May 30, 2020, p. 51.

"Earth worship is at the heart of our ecological crisis. It is precisely the modern devotion to the cult of consumerism which is driving the horrific global scale of environmental destruction."[91]

The idolatry of earth worship blocks the true worship of the Creator God, justice for the poor and oppressed, and the natural harmony of the created order.

Paul's statement that "God's eternal power and divine nature have been clearly seen and understood from what has been made so that all people are without any excuse." (Romans 1:20) point to our need to safeguard all of creation. Paul then adds that people's consciences also bear witness to the laws of nature, accusing or defending them (Romans 2:14-16). We are without excuse for the way we manipulate nature for our self-centred reasons.

For example, genetically modified seeds for crops may prove to be one modern source of manipulation. As already mentioned, farmers who use Monsanto seeds may increase the size and frequency of their crops, but the consequence may be to create monstrosities from which there is no return. Farmers suffer from not being able to replant their own seed. Nepal is one country that has so far forbidden Monsanto from entering the country.

The church must now become "the conscience of the nation," pointing to moral values as the only way to peace and happiness and to the just use of natural resources. Institutionally the church itself should be seen to be a moral society. Its buildings and grounds need to reflect kingdom values, as does its care for suffering people and for the "groaning and frustration of nature." But the will to act compassionately and justly needs the empowering presence of the Holy Spirit in all they try to do.

In one church I briefly served in New Zealand the members, who were largely of Pacific Island heritage, were inspired to plough up a field behind the church, plant vegetables, and then barter them in the nearby market, a practice they were already familiar with in their original culture. But for a church to make an impact in renewing its neighbourhood, it needs to be a prophetic voice for compassion and justice, costly as this may prove to be.

Christian NGOs are also agents for the renewal of creation. The relief and development work of agencies such as World Vision, Tearfund, World Relief Commission and many church-sponsored NGOs, including the Catholic Caritas, have made a significant contribution to meeting human need.

---

91   Michael Northcote, "The Spirit of Environmentalism" in *The Care of Creation* by R J Berry, p. 168.

I am impressed with the practical support Barnabas Fund gives to perse-cuted Christians throughout the developing world. A Rocha is another global movement emphasising the restoration of wetlands and the protec-tion of birds, animals and native plants life.

Ultimately the renewal of earth depends on renewing both religious and social values. The Gospel challenges us all to repent of our selfish life-styles and to put our trust in God to renew his world.

More than 50 years ago, the Lausanne Covenant of 1974 stated: "All of us are shocked by the poverty of millions and disturbed by the injustices that cause it. Those of us who live in affluent circumstances accept our duty to develop a simple lifestyle in order to contribute more generously to both relief and evangelism" (para 9). Unfortunately, evangelical Chris-tians and their churches have done little to make this duty a reality during these years

We agree that there is no one definition of a simple lifestyle, for people live at different social and economic levels. But we can all live more simply with a concern for love and justice for those suffering from poverty and oppression. We restate Jesus' commission is to love God with our whole being and to love our neighbours as ourselves. This means we don't really love God if we don't at the same time love and serve our neighbour. Gen-erosity in tithing or giving to the needs of others is one indication of our being purposeful stewards.

As Christians we may not belong to the world, but God has put us in it to be both a serving community and a prophetic voice for his kingdom, to safeguard it and restore it on earth to his glory.

Conclusion

We endorse the general agreement among scientists that the rising level of greenhouse gases in the atmosphere is directly influencing the rise and fall of global temperatures.

We call for more research on the relative influence of each of the constituent gases, namely carbon dioxide, methane, ozone and water vapour; also on the relative influence of the sun's radiation, sun spots, volcanic activity, and the influence of clouds, wind and rain on temperatures. We urge the so-called alarmists and sceptics to begin talking and listening to one another.

For most of the world, adapting to climate change is still possible. The extremes of climate may be cyclic, as in past history. We need to adapt to these rather than panic, for God the Creator will not allow evil and demonic forces to destroy his beloved planet.

We appeal to individuals and their families to affirm that the environment is our common home, to be shared with all creation. Together we depend on each other, human beings and animals.

As followers of Jesus, we are called to be the light of the world and the salt of the earth, and to ascend the hill of the Lord with clean hands and a pure heart. For this we pray.

We appeal to our churches and their mission agencies to be compassionate to all who suffer. We must be prophets of justice for the harmony and the unity of national societies, and priests interceding for the healing of the frustrated natural world. We take seriously the maxim, "When Christians take the earth seriously, people will take the gospel seriously."

We appeal to nations to rebuke the consumerism and greed of those who unjustly rule over them. We call them to regular days of rest and worship, to restore those falsely imprisoned, and to work for the lessening of poverty. We recognise that sustaining and renewing the earth is God's gift to all who live on it.

We end this appeal for the care of God's creation with God's words to Solomon during the dedication of the Temple:

> "If my people who are called by my name will humble themselves and pray and seek my face and turn from their wicked ways, then I will hear from heaven and will forgive their sin and will heal their land" (2 Chronicles 7:14).

Amen!

Selected Bibliography

Atkinson, David, The Message of Genesis 1-11 (Leicester: Inter-Varsity Press, 1990)

Beaver, R Pierce, et al., consulting editors, Eerdman's Handbook to the World's Religions (Grand Rapids: Eerdmans, 1982)

Berry, R J, ed., The Care of Creation (Leicester: Inter-Varsity Press, 2000)

Bookless, Dave, Planetwise (London: A Rocha International, 2017)

Church of England Mission and Public Affairs Council, Sharing God's Planet: a Christian vision for a sustainable future (London: Church House publishing, 2005)

De Witt, Calvin, ed., The Environment and the Christian (Grand Rapids, MI: Baker Book House, 1991)

Gnanakan, Ken, Responsible Stewardship of God's Creation (Bonn: Cultural and Science Publications, 2014)

Green, Michael, The Message of Matthew (Leicester: Inter-Varsity Press, 2000)

Hallman. David G., ed. Ecotheology: Voices from South and North (Maryknoll, NY: Orbis Books, 1994)

Hoggard Creegan, Nicola and Shepherd, Andrew, eds. Creation and Hope, (Eugene, OR: Pickwick, 2018)

Granberg-Michaelson, Wesley, ed. Tending the Garden: Essays on the Gospel and the Earth (Grand Rapids: Eerdmans, 1990)

Hollinghurst, Steve, New Age Paganism and Christian Mission (Cambridge, UK: Grove Books, 2003)

Küng, Hans, On Being a Christian (Glasgow: Collins, 1978)

McFague, Sally, A New Climate for Theology: God, the World, and Global Warming (Philadelphia: Fortress Press, 2008)

Mission and Public Affairs Council of the Anglican Church, Sharing God's Planet: a Christian vision for a sustainable future (London, Church House Publishing, 2005)

Mosley, Michael and Spencer, Mimi, The Fast Diet (NY: Simon and Schuster, 2015)

Musk, Bill, Touching the Soul of Islam (Crowborough, UK, MARC, 1995)

Nicholls, Bruce J, ed. In Word and Deed (Exeter: Paternoster Press, 1985)

Nicholls, Bruce, Is There Hope for Planet Earth? An ethical response to climate change (Manila: Asia Theological Association, 2010)

Nicholls, Bruce, Building Bridges from Asian Faiths to Jesus in the Gospels (Oxford: Regnum Publishers, 2019)

Partridge, Christopher H. ed. Dictionary of Contemporary Religion in the Western World (Leicester: Inter Varsity Press, 2002)

Philip, T V, Krishna Mohan Banerjea, Christian Apologist (Madras: CLS, 1982)

Ro, Bong and Nicholls, Bruce, Beyond Creation, (Oxford: Regnum Publishers, 1992)

Shapiro, Judith, Mao's War Against Nature: Politics and the Environment in Revolutionary China (Cambridge, UK: University Press, 2001)

Schirrmacher, Thomas and Johnson, Thomas K, Creation Care and Loving Our Neighbours: studies in environmental ethics. (Bonn: Hänssler Verlag, 2016)

Simiyu, Stella, and Harris, Peter, Caring for Creation (Cambridge: Grove Books, 2008).

Tripp, Dick, Caring for Creation (Wellington: Avery Bartlett, 2011)

Wilkinson, David, The Message of Creation (Leicester: Inter Varsity Press, 2002)

Wright, Christopher J H, The Mission of God (Nottingham: Inter-Varsity Press, 2006)

General Index

World Evangelical Alliance

World Evangelical Alliance is a global ministry working with local churches around the world to join in common concern to live and proclaim the Good News of Jesus in their communities. WEA is a network of churches in 129 nations that have each formed an evangelical alliance and over 100 international organizations joining together to give a worldwide identity, voice and platform to more than 600 million evangelical Christians. Seeking holiness, justice and renewal at every level of society – individual, family, community and culture, God is glorified and the nations of the earth are forever transformed.

Christians from ten countries met in London in 1846 for the purpose of launching, in their own words, "a new thing in church history, a definite organization for the expression of unity amongst Christian individuals belonging to different churches." This was the beginning of a vision that was fulfilled in 1951 when believers from 21 countries officially formed the World Evangelical Fellowship. Today, 150 years after the London gathering, WEA is a dynamic global structure for unity and action that embraces 600 million evangelicals in 129 countries. It is a unity based on the historic Christian faith expressed in the evangelical tradition. And it looks to the future with vision to accomplish God's purposes in discipling the nations for Jesus Christ.

Commissions:

- Theology
- Missions
- Religious Liberty
- Women's Concerns
- Youth
- Information Technology

Initiatives and Activities

- Ambassador for Human Rights
- Ambassador for Refugees
- Creation Care Task Force
- Global Generosity Network
- International Institute for Religious Freedom
- International Institute for Islamic Studies
- Leadership Institute
- Micah Challenge
- Global Human Trafficking Task Force
- Peace and Reconciliation Initiative
- UN-Team

Church Street Station
P.O. Box 3402
New York, NY 10008-3402
Phone +[1] 212 233 3046
Fax +[1] 646-957-9218
www.worldea.org

WEA
World Evangelical Alliance

International Institute for Religious Freedom

Purpose and Aim

The "International Institute for Religious Freedom" (IIRF) is a network of professors, researchers, academics, specialists and university institutions from all continents with the aim of working towards:

- The establishment of reliable facts on the restriction of religious freedom worldwide.
- The making available of results of such research to other researchers, politicians, advocates, as well as the media.
- The introduction of the subject of religious freedom into academic research and curricula.
- The backing up of advocacy for victims of violations of religious freedom in the religious, legal and political world.
- Serving discriminated and persecuted believers and academics wherever they are located. Publications and other research will be made available as economically and as readily available as possible to be affordable in the Global South.

Tools

The IIRF encourages all activities that contribute to the understanding of religious freedom. These include:

- Dissemination of existing literature, information about archives, compilation of bibliographies etc.
- Production and dissemination of new papers, journals and books.
- Gathering and analysis of statistics and evidence.
- Supplying of ideas and materials to universities and institutions of theological education to encourage the inclusion of religious freedom issues into curricula.
- Guiding postgraduate students in research projects either personally or in cooperation with the universities and educational institutions.
- Representation at key events where opportunity is given to strengthen connections with the wider religious liberty community and with politicians, diplomats and media.

Online / Contact:

- www.iirf.eu / info@iirf.eu

Institute of Islamic Studies

The protestant "Institute of Islamic Studies" is a network of scholars in Islamic studies and is carried out by the Evangelical Alliance in Germany, Austria and Switzerland.

Churches, the political arena, and society at large are provided foundational information relating to the topic of 'Islam' through research and the presentation thereof via publications, adult education seminars, and democratic political discourse.

Research Focus

As far as our work is concerned, the focus is primarily on Islam in Europe, the global development of Islamic theology and of Islamic fundamentalism, as well as a respectful and issue-related meeting of Christians and Muslims. In the process, misunderstandings about Islam and Muslims can be cleared up, and problematic developments in Islamic fundamentalism and political Islam are explained. Through our work we want to contribute to engaging Muslims in an informed and fair manner.

What we do

Lectures, seminars, and conferences for public authorities, churches, political audiences, and society at large

- Participation in special conferences on the topic of Islam
- The publication of books in German, English, and Spanish
- The preparation of scholarly studies for the general public
- Special publications on current topics
- Production of a German-English journal entitled "Islam and Christianity"
- Regular press releases with commentaries on current events from a scholarly Islamic studies perspective
- Academic surveys and experts' reports for advisory boards of government
- Regular news provided as summaries of Turkish and Arab language internet publications
- Fatwa archive
- Website with a collection of articles

Giving Hands

GIVING HANDS GERMANY (GH) was established in 1995 and is officially recognized as a nonprofit foreign aid organization. It is an international operating charity that – up to now – has been supporting projects in about 40 countries on four continents. In particular we care for orphans and street children. Our major focus is on Africa and Central America. GIVING HANDS always mainly provides assistance for self-help and furthers human rights thinking.

The charity itself is not bound to any church, but on the spot we are co-operating with churches of all denominations. Naturally we also cooperate with other charities as well as governmental organizations to provide assistance as effective as possible under the given circumstances.

The work of GIVING HANDS GERMANY is controlled by a supervisory board. Members of this board are Manfred Feldmann, Colonel V. Doner and Kathleen McCall. Dr. Christine Schirrmacher is registered as legal manager of GIVING HANDS at the local district court. The local office and work of the charity are coordinated by Rev. Horst J. Kreie as executive manager. Dr. theol. Thomas Schirrmacher serves as a special consultant for all projects.

Thanks to our international contacts companies and organizations from many countries time and again provide containers with gifts in kind which we send to the different destinations where these goods help to satisfy elementary needs. This statutory purpose is put into practice by granting nutrition, clothing, education, construction and maintenance of training centers at home and abroad, construction of wells and operation of water treatment systems, guidance for self-help and transportation of goods and gifts to areas and countries where needy people live.

GIVING HANDS has a publishing arm under the leadership of Titus Vogt, that publishes human rights and other books in English, Spanish, Swahili and other languages.

These aims are aspired to the glory of the Lord according to the basic Christian principles put down in the Holy Bible.

Baumschulallee 3a • D-53115 Bonn • Germany
Phone: +49 / 228 / 695531 • Fax +49 / 228 / 695532
www.gebende-haende.de • info@gebende-haende.de

Martin Bucer Seminary

Faithful to biblical truth
Cooperating with the Evangelical Alliance
Reformed

Solid training for the Kingdom of God
- Alternative theological education
- Study while serving a church or working another job
- Enables students to remain in their own churches
- Encourages independent thinking
- Learning from the growth of the universal church.

Academic
- For the Bachelor's degree: 180 Bologna-Credits
- For the Master's degree: 120 additional Credits
- Both old and new teaching methods: All day seminars, independent study, term papers, etc.

Our Orientation:
- Complete trust in the reliability of the Bible
- Building on reformation theology
- Based on the confession of the German Evangelical Alliance
- Open for innovations in the Kingdom of God

Our Emphasis:
- The Bible
- Ethics and Basic Theology
- Missions
- The Church

Our Style:
- Innovative
- Relevant to society
- International
- Research oriented
- Interdisciplinary

Structure
- 15 study centers in 7 countries with local partners
- 5 research institutes
- President: Prof. Dr. Thomas Schirrmacher
  Vice President: Prof. Dr. Thomas K. Johnson
- Deans: Thomas Kinker, Th.D.;
  Titus Vogt, lic. theol., Carsten Friedrich, M.Th.

Missions through research
- Institute for Religious Freedom
- Institute for Islamic Studies
- Institute for Life and Family Studies
- Institute for Crisis, Dying, and Grief Counseling
- Institute for Pastoral Care

www.bucer.eu • info@bucer.eu

Berlin | Bielefeld | Bonn | Chemnitz | Hamburg | Munich | Pforzheim

Innsbruck | Istanbul | Izmir | Linz | Prague | São Paulo | Tirana | Zurich